Let One Go F

Hannah Hickman, née Weinberger, was the onl
Weinberger family of Würzburg, Germany. At th
England on a *Kindertransport* shortly before the outbreak of the Second World War in 1939. She was adopted by a young teacher in Bristol, Nell Gill, who cared for and educated her with help from friends, relatives and colleagues. During the war Hannah's father died in hospital, and her mother, brother and sister, as well as other relatives, were deported to Auschwitz.

Hannah Weinberger studied at two British universities, becoming a teacher in grammar schools. After marriage to Aubrey Hickman and raising three children, she taught for some years, then undertook research for a higher degree. By focussing on the writer Robert Musil, a contemporary of her parents and of Hitler, she gained greater understanding of the political situation that had enabled Hitler and the Nazi party to come to power in Germany. Her book *Robert Musil and the Culture of Vienna* was published in 1984 in England and the USA, paperback 1991. From 1977-94 she lectured at the universities of Manchester and Salford, was active in the International Musil Society and worked for international understanding.

Let One Go Free... [is] not simply the story of one child who escaped with the *Kindertransport* to England, but an evocative family portrait with vivid recollections of the life of an assimilated German-Jewish family in Würzburg in the 1930s. Hickman's skills as a researcher enable her to supplement her personal reminiscences with a rich range of historical documentation, including Gestapo records from Würzburg; family letters from the crucial years 1938-43; correspondence with relatives who escaped to the United States; and letters from non-Jewish family friends. Thus the individual narrative opens into a panorama of the social activities of a German-Jewish family.

Through its sensitive handling of a variety of sources this memoir provides a model for an integrated form of life history.

Professor Edward Timms, Director, Centre for German-Jewish Studies, University of Sussex

For us who are fifty years away from the horrors of the Holocaust, and perhaps especially for young people, Hannah Hickman provides a personal story written with careful and graphic simplicity. Histories of the period operate at a different level, but the stories of individuals directly affected by the actions of national leaders and politicians give us a direct picture of what it was like to live then. Hannah Hickman's unpretentious autobiography draws the reader into the experiences of a typical middle-class German family that was riven apart and well-nigh destroyed because it was Jewish. We need to remember such stories.

David Blamires, Professor of German, University of Manchester

Let One Go Free

Hannah Hickman

Let One Go Free

Hannah Hickman

Let One Go Free

Hannah Hickman

Published in Great Britain by
Quill Press
Woodlands, Main Street, Kirton,
Newark, Nottinghamshire. NG22 9LP

© 2003 Quill Press

British Library Catalogue in Publication Data
A catalogue record for this book is available from the British Library

ISBN 0-9543001-0-6

All rights reserved. No part of this publication may be reproduced in any form or by any means, electronic, mechanical, photocopying, recording or otherwise, without the prior permission of the publisher.

Printed and bound by Cromwell Press Ltd, Trowbridge

For my children and grandchildren

and in memory of my grandparents, father, mother, brother and sister

The title is adapted from Isaiah ch. 58 v .6:

"... to let the oppressed go free..."

TABLE OF CONTENTS

Note on Translations

All translations from German are my own. Occasional translator's comments for these texts are given in square brackets [ ].

LIST OF ILLUSTRATIONS

Photographs were taken by members of the family, except where otherwise indicated.

PREFACE

I should like to start by saying that this is a personal memoir, not a history book. The book has been written for my teenage grandchildren and for readers who do not know much about the Holocaust in Germany. I would ask readers to follow the sequence of events regarding my life, and that of my family, as they are given, without being too concerned about historical details.

May I suggest that those would like to have more detail should consult public libraries or history textbooks. Such historical facts as I have included are given only to act as a framework or context for the story of the Weinberger family and of my own life. Much more could have been said, but my aim throughout has been to allow the reader to follow the main story without being distracted.

Hannah Hickman
Winter 2002

Introduction
My Journey to England, June 1939

This is the story of a family, a German-Jewish family in the twentieth century. Some of the things that happened to members of this family happened also to millions of others, but this is not an attempt to write history. It is a personal account, pieced together from recollections, letters and photographs long after the events. It is also an attempt to explain to my children and grandchildren how it came about that I arrived in England on 5 June 1939, a girl of eleven, alone.

On 4 June 1939, my mother woke me about four o'clock in the morning. I hastily got dressed and had breakfast. Then my parents and I left for the railway station in Würzburg, where we lived. Soon the train arrived. It had already called at many cities and was full of children, some as young as three or four years old. My parents were allowed to travel with me for about half an hour, then at the next suitable station they got out and we said goodbye. I remember seeing them walking beside the track as the train pulled away. I never saw them or my brother and sister again.

My journey to England was only made possible by the generous offer of hospitality from Miss Nell Gill, a teacher in Bristol and a friend of my cousin Hanna Jacobsohn. The National Socialist government of Germany was threatening Jewish citizens more and more. Those hoping to emigrate to England and the United States of America were faced by strict immigration regulations; but after *Kristallnacht*, 9 November 1938, when Jewish synagogues, businesses and homes all over Germany were attacked and many Jews arrested and killed, the

British government allowed 10,000 Jewish children to come to England. Many organizations worked extremely hard to make this possible: Jewish associations, the Churches, the Quakers and numerous fearless individuals who arranged transport for the children out of Germany and other countries where their lives were threatened. On arrival in England, the children were settled and cared for by other organizations, unless, as in my case, they already had a private sponsor. The whole operation became known as the *Kindertransports* and as a result of its work, many thousands of children were saved. All of us 'children' owe a deep debt of gratitude for the generosity of the British government.

After the sea crossing from the Hook of Holland to Harwich, we took the train to London. For me, aged eleven, it was a big adventure! One thing I could not understand was that all the towns were apparently called 'Virol'. Years later, I discovered that 'Virol' was a popular health food, prominently advertised at every station.

Finally we arrived in London. At Liverpool Street Station we waited in a gloomy basement hall. When almost all the other children had been collected and I was becoming anxious, suddenly there was the kindly face of Nell's mother, Mrs. Alice Gill, who had had a long journey across London to get to the station. She took me to stay overnight with Nell's sister, Connie Gill, in a flat on Haverstock Hill, Hampstead. There I was visited by my cousin Adolf Jacobsohn, who had lived and studied in England for several years.

The next day, 6 June, Connie put me on the train to Bristol, with a label round my neck and a special request to the guard to keep an eye on me, especially as I knew little English. Nell was waiting for me at Temple Meads Station. It was to be a temporary stay of six months or so, until my parents, brother and sister could complete the formalities to emigrate all together to the USA. But on 3 September 1939 war was declared, and I never saw them again. Yet through the kindness of Nell Gill and her family, and that of many other people, I was able to build up a new life in England.

The fate of the Jews of Europe in the twentieth century has been chronicled and debated by professional historians and others ever since the end of the Second World War. Six million Jews perished. The present memoir is personal and limited in scope. Yet in order to understand what happened, it is necessary to look further back. So it may be best to begin by tracing such members of the family as can be found in the nineteenth century. No attempt is being made to establish factual accuracy in every respect, firstly because this is not a history book, and secondly because even if this were attempted, at least some of the documents would have been destroyed during the war. Wherever possible, however, historical documents have been cited to confirm details of family history. With the aid of such information as I can find, I hope to build up a picture of my grandparents and parents and their life in Germany, going on to my later life in England.

Chapter One

Two German-Jewish Families Before, During and After World War I

This chapter sets the scene for the two families in which my father and mother grew up, Jewish families living in Germany, in many ways typical of their time. I remember my grandparents on both sides very clearly. Further back I have been able to obtain more information about my mother's side than about my father's family. The next generation, my uncles and aunts, formed part of my childhood. Their children, my cousins, were older than I was, and some of them were an essential part of my life both in Germany and later. Several of them are still alive at the time of writing.

Almost all these relatives were affected by the Holocaust, and that is why I am including them in this chapter. I would like to show that the Holocaust was, for people like myself, not a series of distant events acted out by politicians in the capital. It was that as well, but my point is that it was a long process that affected me and all my family every day in every aspect of our lives, as will be seen later in this book. So I would ask you, the reader, to have patience while I describe the members of this greater family, and to realize that what happened to them and to me was part of a national and international pattern. For this reason, too, I have said a little about Jewish life in Europe before the Holocaust, and have sketched in the historical context to the rise of Hitler. Later in the book, there are some short sections outlining the background to life in Nazi Germany and during the Second World War.

My paternal grandparents, Josef and Rosette Weinberger, lived in Bayreuth. Josef was born on 14 March 1861 in the village of Wüstensachsen in the Rhön Mountains in central Germany. He became a master tailor and eventually set up in business in Bayreuth. His wife Rosette, née Badmann, was born on 2 August 1865 in Oettingen, north of Donauwörth on the Danube. They married in the late 1880s and had three sons: Karl, my father (b. 20 October 1889), Max (b. 1893) and Leo (b. 1899). Bayreuth, in north-east Bavaria, near the border with the Czech Republic, was a market centre for the farmers of the surrounding countryside. It became nationally and internationally known when Richard Wagner built the Festival Theatre there, specially designed for performances of his operas. The theatre opened in 1876 and the tradition of Wagner festivals continues to this day.

My grandparents owned a tall, old house at 29 Ludwigstrasse, near the park attached to the palace of the Margraves of Bayreuth. The business premises were on the ground floor, and the living quarters on the first and second floors. My father and his youngest brother Leo both studied law, but Max trained as a tailor like his father, spending some years as an apprentice in Munich, and was a partner in the business.

I remember being driven, probably in 1937, in Max's car with my father from Würzburg to Bayreuth, secretly, at night. The journey is associated in my mind with preparations for the grandparents' Golden Wedding. What impressed me (aged nine) about this journey was first of all going in a car: we always travelled by train, and as far as I knew only doctors and the very rich had cars. When I saw Max again after the war, he told me that the car was needed for his role in the family business: it was his job to drive out into the villages and measure the vicar, the mayor and the schoolmaster for suits, which would then be made in Bayreuth under grandfather's supervision. The other aspect of that car journey that I found exciting was the speed and the darkness, rushing along country roads lit only by the glare of headlamps. I had read a story about Chinese refugees in Manchuria escaping from Japanese invaders at night across a lake in a small boat, and in my imagination our journey was something of the same kind. It says much for my parents' care and their endeavour to give us a 'normal' childhood that at this stage I was completely unaware how true such a comparison would soon become.

Leo, the youngest of the three brothers, was a solicitor in Nuremberg. Whereas Max did not marry until later, Leo's wife Lisel came from a Christian family in one of the small towns along the river Main. Leo and Lisel had no children of their own and often came to visit our family in Würzburg. While the grandparents were Orthodox Jews, their sons' attitude to religion was more liberal. The difference in religious background may have been one reason why Leo and Lisel had no children; yet when I, in my turn, announced my engagement to a Christian, it was Leo who begged me most earnestly to reconsider my decision to 'marry out' of the Jewish community.

It seems unlikely that I shall ever be able to find out anything about my great-grandparents on my father's side. The name Weinberger ('of the vineyard') is fairly common in Jewish circles, and a Czech composer of that name (1896–1967) is known for his opera *Schwanda the Bagpiper*. My grandmother's maiden name, Badmann, translates as 'bath attendant', possibly a reference to the communal baths in the villages for men and women respectively, although a similar word was used in earlier centuries for 'barber' or even 'village doctor'. Jewish life in the *shtetls* (little towns) of eastern and central Europe, up to the early years of the twentieth century, is vividly described in two books originally written in Yiddish, *Burning Candles* by Bella Chagall, wife of the painter Marc Chagall, and in the stories of Sholom Aleichem, *Tevye the Milkman*, on which the musical *Fiddler on the Roof* is based.

Since Jews were forbidden to own land, they had to earn their living in trade, business and the professions. Jewish pedlars would travel from village to village on foot, selling books, cloth, ribbons and whatever could not be produced locally. Once a pedlar became more prosperous, he would settle down and open a shop. Others were moneylenders, tailors, like my grandfather, butchers and so on. In the following generations, there was sometimes enough money to send the sons to university; they then set up in the towns as lawyers, like my father, doctors, or bankers, like my other grandfather. The respect for learning inherent in the Jewish rabbinical tradition led some into philosophy and other branches of scholarship. The great seventeenth century thinker Spinoza was a Jew. In the eighteenth century, Moses Mendelssohn became famous as a philosopher, and his son, father of the composer, is reported to have said: "For years I was regarded simply as the son of my father, and now I am only the father of my son!" The Jewish poet Heinrich Heine (1797–1856), whose poems were set to music by Schubert and Schumann, had to leave his native Germany on account of his political opinions, and spent the last twenty-five years of his life in France.

Jewish communities were spread throughout Europe, except for Spain and Portugal, from which they had been expelled at the end of the fifteenth century. The Jews of Iberian origin are known as Sephardim, while Jews from central and eastern Europe are called Ashkenazim. In Russia they were confined to the western provinces. In the towns, at least until the eighteenth century, Jews had to live in areas known as ghettos. In Austria, a law of 1781 allowed certain freedoms to non-Catholics, such as entry to the state service, and the right to buy land. In addition, Jews no longer had to wear the sign marking them out as Jews, and the ghettos were abolished. Jews were also obliged to take surnames, instead of being known simply as 'son of ...', as in my mother's maiden name, Jacobsohn. Some chose names connected with their occupation, such as Gold or Weinberger, my father's name. Others preferred names derived from their home town, such as Wiener, i.e. of Vienna.

During a thousand years, antisemitism led to much persecution, but at times there was respect and even co-operation. Gradually things began to improve in western Europe, but in Russia treatment of the Jews by the state authorities was cruel and inhuman, culminating in the pogroms of 1881. In the following years, hundreds of thousands of Jews fled from Russia. Many were received by Jewish communities already established in western Europe, the British dominions and the New World. One of those who went to the United States as a young woman became the late Prime Minister of Israel, Golda Meir. Two other figures who emigrated at this time were Louis Mayer, one of the founders of Hollywood, and Michael Marks, the co-founder of Marks and Spencer.

* * *

My maternal grandparents, Moritz and Betty Jacobsohn, lived in Lüneburg in northern Germany, south of Hamburg. Moritz was born on 1 December 1845, in Nienburg on the river Weser, between Hanover and Bremen. His parents were Anselm and Sara Jacobsohn. Anselm was a hide merchant. The earliest known ancestor of the family moved to Nienburg in 1767 from the village of Obertheres, near Hassfurt on the river Main, south of the Rhön Mountains. He or one of his family was Court Jew to one of the aristocratic houses of the area. Court Jews were employed at this period by German princes, large and small, as business and financial managers; they were often very successful, but had no rights of their own. So both my paternal grandfather and the earliest known ancestor on my mother's side came from the Rhön area.

About a hundred years after my great-grandparents died, I was given valuable information about them by Frau Christa

Stellmann, a friend of my cousin Hanna Jacobsohn (later Naumann). Christa and her son made a special journey to Nienburg, to the Jewish cemetery. She took photographs of the tombstones and found a German text on one face, a Hebrew text on the other:

a) 'Anselm M. Jacobsohn, born in Nienburg 3 June 1801, died 6 March 1887. Blessed be his memory.'

b) 'Frau Sara Jacobsohn, born in Braunschweig 2 January 1808, died in Nienburg 18 October 1889. Her life was filled with love and caring.'

But the Hebrew text could not be translated by myself or my cousin. Very fortunately, her eldest granddaughter, Mäggy, who then lived in Israel, was on a rare visit home and translated the Hebrew inscriptions:

a) 'Here lies a man who steadfastly followed his path with an upright heart: Asher ben Menachem. We will honour the memory of his name.'

b) 'A good mother to her family with warmth and uprightness and cheerfulness in her heart. Sara: she was a light for her husband Asher. May she live on in us.'

Their son, my grandfather Moritz, moved to Lüneburg in 1860 and became a banker. During the war against France of 1870–71 he fought in the Prussian army, was wounded in battle and promoted to officer in recognition of his courage in the face of the enemy.

Lüneburg was an ancient town important for its salt deposits, and a market centre. In the Middle Ages it was a member of the Hanseatic League, a confederation of cities around the Baltic Sea with considerable power. The main streets of the town were lined with the tall, gable-fronted houses typical of northern Europe. As a young man the composer Johann Sebastian Bach spent some years as a chorister there, and was impressed by the virtuoso playing of the organist at St. John's Church. My grandparents' house stood quite near this church, whose spire could be seen from the garden.

My grandmother, Betty Jacobsohn, was born in Lüneburg on 15 March 1859; her parents were Markus and Henriette Heinemann. Markus was a merchant with a house in the centre of the town, and they had seventeen children, of whom several died in infancy. Betty and Moritz married in 1877. This was a period of growing prosperity in Germany. Bismarck, Prime Minister of Prussia, had succeeded in uniting the many smaller German states under Prussia's leadership, largely as a result of the war against France. In the following years, Germany, whose development had lagged behind that of the western powers, rapidly established herself as a modern industrial nation.

My grandparents were actively involved in the life of Lüneburg. Grandfather was a co-founder of the Officers' Association, and for two four-year periods, president of the Jewish congregation. Grandmother was on the committee of the Patriotic Women's Association. During the First World War she was asked to take charge of catering services at the railway station for troops passing through, and later for refugees from the former East Prussia.

Moritz and Betty had six children altogether. The first five were born in steady succession up to 1886: Martha (1878), Hermann (1879), Albert (1881), Elisabeth (1882) and Adolf (1886). Then, after an interval of fourteen years, my mother Ruth was born on 17 February 1900. Martha married a doctor, Max Meyer, and they had three children, Lisi, Lotte and a son, Heinz, who died young. Hermann married Margarethe Flemming, daughter of a Gentile doctor; they had four children, Helmuth, Lore, Hanna and Adolf. Hermann became Professor for Comparative Philology at the university of Marburg on the river Lahn, Germany's oldest Protestant university. Elisabeth (Lieschen) married Dr. Siegfried Levinger; they had a son, Fritz, and a daughter, Ruth. Albert died relatively young of a brain tumour in 1912. Adolf volunteered for war service in the First World War, became a lieutenant and died in action in Flanders on 17 March 1918.

This was a typical Jewish middle-class family whose members carried out their work and took part in public life, seeing themselves as in no way different from their Gentile neighbours, apart from religion.

The causes of the First World War were many and complex. Germany was still trying to become the equal of the great imperial nations with their colonies. She had a treaty with Austria-Hungary, a multi-national empire presided over by the aged Emperor Francis Joseph I, which was seething with discontented nationalist groups. The Balkan wars of 1912–13 had led to a potentially explosive situation in Serbia, Bosnia and neighbouring states. The assassination of the heir to the Austrian throne by a Serb nationalist, at Sarajevo on 28 June 1914, led to the outbreak of war on 4 August, with Austria and Germany fighting against Serbia and Russia in the east, at the same time as against France and Great Britain in the west and Italy in the south. In 1917, the United States of America joined the western powers against Germany. After millions of casualties and much suffering on all sides, an armistice was finally signed on 11 November 1918.

* * *

The lives of both my parents were affected by the four years of war. When it broke out, my mother was fourteen years old, and eight months before it ended her beloved brother Adolf had died in action. My father was twenty-four in June 1914, a law student; to judge by dated photographs he must have volunteered for military service from the start. His brother Max, four years younger, also joined the army, as did the youngest, Leo, when he was old enough. The misery and brutality of trench warfare has been poignantly described by writers and poets of the time. The Austrian writer Robert Musil kept a diary during his war service on the Italian front, in which vivid descriptions of dangerous incidents alternate with reflective passages. He records the euphoria that greeted the outbreak of war, but also the grim litany of names of the dead, which "must rend the nation apart, one of those suppressed experiences which avenge themselves as hysteria" – a prophetic comment, the truth of which was soon to become apparent.

By the end of the war in November 1918, Europe was fundamentally changed. In Russia, the Tsar had been deposed in 1917 and a Bolshevik republic proclaimed; the entire imperial family was assassinated in 1918. In Austria, the old Emperor had died in 1916. His successor, Charles I, abdicated in November 1918, when an Austrian republic was declared. In October 1918 an independent Czechoslovak republic was established, and in the Balkans various groups also claimed their independence. The German military leaders finally demanded an armistice. At the same time, in various parts of Germany, revolutionary, Soviet-style sailors', soldiers' and workers' councils assumed control, leading to political and economic chaos. The German Emperor abdicated and Germany, too, became a republic in 1918. In the space of only two years, Russia, Austria and Germany, three great empires each symbolized by eagles, had collapsed: truly, as has been said, the Fall of Eagles.

So how did the political and economic situation in Germany affect my parents at the time they met? The years after the First World War were marked by instability, inflation, hunger and resentment. It would be true to say that the period when my parents met, married and when I was born was also the period leading up to the Holocaust. Hitler did not arise out of a vacuum, but out of the whole German situation after the First World War. My parents lived in this unstable time, which affected them as much as everyone else. For example, they did not marry until four years after their engagement, and I, their first child, was not born until five years after that.

The new German *Republican* National Assembly convened in 1919 at Weimar, formerly the home of Goethe, revered as Germany's greatest poet, and a new constitution was drawn up. The majority of votes went to the Republican parties. Yet neither the people nor their representatives had any experience of democracy, and Parliament soon came to be dominated by parties hostile to a democratic state. From 1918 to 1920, political instability continued. Early in 1918, Germany had imposed punitive peace terms on Russia. When the peace treaty of Germany and Austria with France, Great Britain and the USA was drawn up, its terms were equally harsh. France's implacable resentment after her humiliation by Germany in 1871 prevailed over the less punitive terms proposed by the USA. The treaty was signed at Versailles in 1919.

At some time towards the end of the war, my uncle Max had found himself in Lüneburg with his army unit. He seems to have met my grandfather Moritz, perhaps at the synagogue, and received an invitation to visit the family. In due course my father also paid a visit to the Jacobsohns and met their youngest daughter. Ruth was nineteen in February 1919, and Karl was thirty in October of that year. Sometime in 1919 my parents became engaged.

1919 may be described as a significant moment: the year when antisemitism became a generally accepted myth. The German people felt their leaders had failed them. They could not understand how, after sustained proclamations of the coming victory, military collapse and defeat had been possible. The right-wing parties argued that it must have been due to treachery: the 'stab in the back' of Jews, Pacifists and Social Democrats. The people's many sacrifices were seen to have been in vain. In addition, hunger and prolonged malnutrition led in 1919 to a severe 'flu epidemic in Germany and Austria, in which many thousands died.

★ ★ ★

During the four years before my parents' marriage in 1923, my father began his career as a lawyer. He had studied at the universities of Leipzig and Passau, and may have needed further training after his army service. He entered the state service as a lawyer and eventually became a public prosecutor.

My mother was still at school in 1919, studying for the German equivalent of the GCE Advanced level examination. After this she studied economics at the universities of Hamburg, Munich and Marburg, but, so far as I know, did not complete a degree course. She was highly gifted as a pianist, played the violin and loved to sing folksongs. In Marburg she often visited her brother Hermann and his wife Grete. Their three eldest children were only a few years younger than herself, and a particularly close relationship grew up between them.

The fact that my parents were engaged for four years before they could think of marriage must have been partly due to my father's need to establish himself in his profession. My mother probably did not think of her studies in terms of a career. But in addition to personal considerations, they had to contend with external circumstances. The economic condition of Germany grew steadily worse, leading to catastrophic levels of inflation. The war effort had been financed not by increasing taxes, but by printing paper money without real financial backing. The huge amounts of reparations Germany had to pay to the victorious Allies under the Versailles Peace Treaty drained her remaining financial reserves. As a result, money became virtually worthless. Butter cost 15,000 marks a pound, and a loaf of bread 2,500 marks. Workers were paid twice a day, then they had half an hour free to rush to the shops to buy food, for by the end of the day prices might have doubled. Savings and pensions lost their value, and there was mass unemployment.

As a result, millions of Germans who had passively accepted the transition from Empire to Republic suffered untold poverty and misery that shattered their faith in the democratic process and left them alienated. At the beginning of 1923, after a long dispute concerning the war reparations, French and Belgian troops occupied the Ruhr area, the centre of German heavy industry. There seemed to be no end to Germany's troubles. More and more people were looking for someone to blame. They wanted a strong leader to make the country great again.

In Bavaria in southern Germany, the political situation was confused. On the one hand, Communist sympathisers were active once more. On the other, nationalist groups led by former officers were becoming increasingly vocal. The antisemitic and anti-Western attitudes of these groups were fuelled by books such as *The Decay of the West*. The author, Oswald Spengler, proclaimed a vision of a resurgent Germany leading a triumphant military crusade against the old nations of the West. Democracy was labelled a sign of weakness. Truth and justice would in future be overcome by vitality and power.

This kind of language is hard to take seriously now, but it was indeed what some Germans wanted to hear. Defeat, reparations, chaotic inflation, hunger and instability created the conditions for acceptance of such calls. In 1923 the officers' groups joined forces with the National Socialist Workers' Party, led by a young Austrian called Adolf Hitler. Hitler was born in the same year as my father (1889) and both went through the horrors of the First World War. In November 1923 there was widespread support for a Nationalist revolution in Munich. At the last moment, most of the leaders decided to wait and see. Hitler, however, chose to go ahead, and on 8 November in Munich led his Nazi troopers in the Beer Hall Putsch. The next morning, the Bavarian police captured Hitler and imprisoned him, along with his closest associates.

The most successful political leader of the Weimar republic, Gustav Stresemann, had brought in measures to end the inflation. Thus 1923 was followed by economic recovery and some improvement in political stability. Through the Pact of Locarno (1925), Germany regained political equality and was allowed to join the League of Nations, a mark of renewed international respectability.

But Hitler, imprisoned in the fortress of Landsberg, had been writing *Mein Kampf* (*My Struggle*), in which he set out his political programme. Among its chief points, reiterated in constant speeches after his release, were opposition to Communism, denunciation of the Versailles Treaty, and hatred of the Jews, who were accused both of being the real force behind Communism and at the same time of being the foreign capitalists who were exploiting defeated Germany.

Chapter Two

In Hitler's Shadow – A Young Family is Established

My parents were married on 12 August 1923 in Lüneburg. My father was then working in Berlin and they began their life together in a small flat there. Although both of them came from relatively prosperous families, the inflation meant that they could barely afford the basic furniture to set up home: two beds, a table and two chairs.

In the cities a wave of gaiety and dancing grew up, as people sought to forget their problems. As conditions gradually improved, the government encouraged artists, dramatists and intellectuals to express themselves freely, in contrast to the censorship of the Wilhelmine empire. Yet the population as a whole still bitterly resented the defeat and the Versailles Treaty. Hitler, by his gifts as a magnetic speaker and clever organizer, was able to capture the leadership of the various small groups that aimed to make Germany strong again. Their hatred of the Jews ignored the fact that for the previous hundred years they had been accepted as citizens, playing a full part in business and the professions and also taking on the obligations of citizenship by fighting for Germany in war. The Jews, and to a lesser extent the Communists, were seen as responsible for all Germany's troubles.

By 1929, Hitler's National Socialist German Workers' Party (NSDAP), having already gained support from conservative quarters, also obtained financial help from heavy industry. The great landowners and industrialists shared Hitler's antisemitic and anti-Communist views. However, in 1929 a world economic crisis, starting in the USA, affected European countries as well. In the Weimar Republic unemployment rose immediately, and it seemed that the country's economy would collapse once more. The effect on recruitment to the Nazi party was remarkable. From 12 seats in the Reichstag (Parliament) in 1928, their strength rose to 107 seats in 1930. At the election of July 1932, the Nazis obtained 230 seats, the largest number of any party.

By this time serious divisions had arisen between the aged President, Paul von Hindenburg, and members of the Republican government. Normal democratic government was no longer working. On 30 January 1933 the President and his senior ally, Franz von Papen, invited Hitler, as head of the largest party, to form a new cabinet. They thought they could use him as a figurehead while carrying out their own Nationalist policies. Hitler soon proved them wrong.

* * *

By the time I was born on 3 February 1928, my father was working in Hof, a small town close to the Czech border. I remember nothing about this place, since by the time I was one and a half years old, my father had been moved to Würzburg, a historic university city on the river Main. This was our home until I emigrated and the rest of the family perished.

For my Weinberger grandparents I was their first grandchild, but none of their letters from this period survive. My Jacobsohn grandparents were thrilled to have a new grandchild after such a long time. They wrote to my mother for her birthday, not long after my birth:

Lüneburg, 16 February 1928

My dear, dear Ruth,

Tomorrow it will already be 28 years, almost three decades, since you came to us as our baby. From that day onwards the sun shone on our house every day, you were not only our joy but also that of your brothers and sisters, who at that time were still gathered around us for many years. And then when heavy clouds darkened our skies and days of deep grief came, then it was our baby who most helped us not to abandon ourselves to what we had lost. And now joy has come to us again through your child, dear Ruth, and we wish you most warmly that with her the same joy may also enter your lives, starting with your new year of life, as for us then. And stay healthy, that is the most important thing. You can imagine how dearly I would love to be with you now for a short visit. You spoiled us from the start with your dear letters, now we always watch out for them with longing. For example I don't yet know if you are home, if you have been out of bed already, if the little, still nameless one has already gained weight and is laughing in her dreams.

You surely received our long letter with the announcement of our birthday gifts, and we would be glad to know if you would like to have the money sent there? But so that your birthday table shall not be quite without gifts from Lüneburg, we have sent you two candlesticks, as a further memento of your family home, and – a large salami sausage, not so much for a memento as to be consumed. To both of you: be happy on the day, healthy and content. In the evening we shall drink a glass of wine to your health and that of your family, and think a lot about you. More than we usually do is indeed hardly possible. If the weather allows, I go into the garden twice a day for half an hour, to breathe the fresh air for which I long. Otherwise I am always at home. But I have had frequent visitors, and as I read a good deal and also do a little embroi-

dery, the day soon passes. Has the chair arrived safely? Where will it stand? You wrote that you had received many congratulations on the birth of your daughter, now you will have to read a great many tomorrow, and so I take my leave with a loving kiss, also for the little one, and repeated, warmest wishes and greetings for all.

With warmest love, your Mother.

And there was a message from grandfather:

My dear, dear Ruth!

For your birthday I send you my very best wishes; may your new year of life be a happy one, may God's blessing go with you and your little one in all your ways. You will all spend a happy day, perhaps already at home. So that you receive this letter in time, it must go to the station, so again warmest greetings to you, Karl and Fräulein Ditha [A friend of my mother's who had come to help].

With warmest love, Father.

My cousin Hanna, 17 years older than myself, wrote to me after the war recalling with some amusement grandfather's reaction to my birth:

Oberlin, Ohio, USA
1 December 1947

My dear Hannah

Today was our grandfather's birthday, he would have been 102... I wish you could visit me and we could talk about the family. Your mother and I often sat up at night talking about our ancestors. I can see the scene so clearly in my mind as if it had been yesterday: you were lying in your pram in the dining-room in Lüneburg, and our old grandfather was bending over you singing soldiers' songs which he had sung in the war of 1870/71, and which he liked so much.

Here is a summary of my birth certificate, see page 27:

Hof, 9 February 1928. Today the district court judge Karl Weinberger gave notice that his wife Ruth Weinberger, née Jacobsohn, had given birth to a girl on 3 February 1928, and that the child had not yet been given a first name.

Additional paragraph (left): Hof, 10 March 1928. Karl Weinberger gave notice that the child had been given the first names Hannah Gertrud.

Additional paragraph (lower left): Hof, 17 January 1939. The father of the child has given notice that she also bears the first name Sara. [By 1939 all Jewish men were required to add 'Israel' to their names, all women to add 'Sara'.]

Some of my earliest memories are associated with Lüneburg. My grandparents owned a spacious house with a beautiful garden near the centre of the town. Grandfather was over eighty when I was born. In his working days he may have kept a carriage, for there were stable-like buildings across the courtyard. Later these were let to a seed-merchant, and I clearly remember the strange smells rising from the sacks of grass seed and various other kinds of seed. The large Alsatian dog kept by the grandparents frightened me; he was probably larger than I was! Grandmother had a beautiful set of porcelain fruit dishes, with a different fruit

My mother, Ruth Jacobsohn, and her mother, Betty Jacobsohn, Lüneburg, 1900

My maternal grandfather, Moritz Jacobsohn, Lüneburg, 1932

The home of my maternal grandparents, the Jacobsohns, in Lüneburg

Josef and Rosette Weinberger, my paternal grandparents, Würzburg, 1938

My mother, Ruth Jacobsohn, on her way to school, Lüneburg, 1908?

My father, Karl Weinberger, in the First World War

Beglaubigte Abschrift aus dem Geburtsregister des Standesamts Hof.

~~Geburtsurkunde.~~

f, am 10. März 1928.
r dem unterzeichneten
andesbeamten erschien
ute, der Persönlichkeit
ch bekannt, der Amts-
chter Karl Weinberger,
hnhaft in Hof, Zeppe-
nstraße 11, und zeigte
, daß dem nebenbezeich-
ten Kinde die Vornamen
nnah Gertrud beigelegt
rden seien.
rgelesen, genehmigt
d unterschrieben.
Karl Weinberger.

Der Standesbeamte.
In Vertretung:
Ordnung.

f, den 17. Januar 1939.
r Kindsvater hat als
setzlicher Vertreter
s nebenbezeichneten
ndes angezeigt, daß
eses zusätzlich den
rnamen Sara führe.
Der Standesbeamte.
Ordnung.

Aa.

Nr. 69.

Hof, am 9. Februar 1928.

Vor dem unterzeichneten Standesbeamten erschien heute, der Persönlichkeit nach durch den von Person bekannten Stadtsekretär Heinrich Hoffmann in Hof anerkannt, der Amtsrichter Karl Weinberger,

wohnhaft in Hof, Zeppelinstraße 11, und zeigte an, daß von der Ruth Weinberger, geborenen Jacobsohn, seiner Ehefrau,

wohnhaft bei ihm,

zu Hof, Biengäßchen 5,

am dritten Februar des Jahres tausend neunhundert achtundzwanzig nachmittags um ein einviertel Uhr ein Mädchen geboren worden sei und daß das Kind einen Vornamen noch nicht erhalten habe.

Vorgelesen, genehmigt und unterschrieben.

Karl Weinberger.

Der Standesbeamte.

In Vertretung: Ordnung.

My Birth Certificate

My father, Karl Weinberger, with baby Hannah, 1928

Hanna Jacobsohn, aged 22, Hannah Weinberger (4), Michael (10 months), Würzburg, 1932

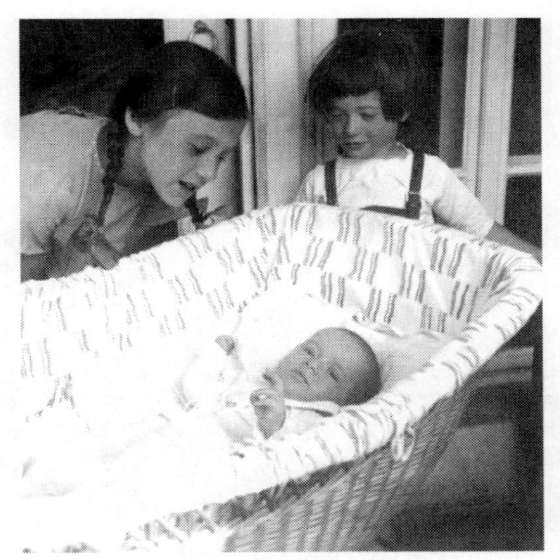

Hannah (left), baby Lies and Micheli, 1936

My mother, Ruth Weinberger, with Lies, 1937

The Weinberger family, 1938, at Kreuzberg, Rhön; left to right: Hannah, Ruth, Lies, father Karl and Micheli. Photo taken by Irene Hilb

My brother, Micheli Weinberger, in the 1930s

Hannah Weinberger, 1937

painted on each one. Sometimes, for a treat, she would hide chocolate beetles and frogs on the veranda for the grandchildren to find.

Grandfather loved to drive out into the country. When we came to visit in the summer, he would sometimes order a small, open horse-carriage, and off we would go, grandparents, mother (my father was not always free to come to Lüneburg), and myself aged two or three, for a day on Lüneburg Heath. This is an extensive moorland area to the west of the town, covered with heather, birch and juniper trees, and famous for its honey.

Another Lüneburg memory relates to a winter visit, about the time of my fifth birthday (3.2.1933). I was wearing a cornflower-blue woollen dress, and my little brother Michael, fourteen months old, wore a toddler's outfit of the same material, probably a gift from grandmother. During a walk not far from the house we met friends. Even at that young age, I was very struck by the serious and concerned expressions of all the adults. It must have been shortly after Hitler had become Chancellor on 30 January, and clearly news of his intentions was spreading fast.

My brother Michael was born on 15 September 1931 in Würzburg. One of the Marburg cousins, Lore, came to help my mother and presumably also looked after me. Similarly, when my sister Elisabeth was born on 14 February 1936, the other cousin, Hanna, came to help. For this and other reasons I always felt closest to the Marburg relations. We visited them too, for instance at Christmas 1937.

* * *

In spite of increasing Nazi domination, my parents succeeded in giving us a happy and stable childhood. At first we lived in a fairly small flat in a semicircular block built for civil servants at Wittelsbacherstrasse, Würzburg (it is still there). A girl from the country came to live with us to help with the housework. Mother was very keen to provide healthy food with plenty of fresh fruit, and rented an allotment where she grew vegetables. My memory of the dry, almost bitter smell of tomatoes straight off the plant dates from this time.

At weekends, if the weather was good, we would go out for the day, taking the train to Gemünden, downstream on the river Main, then make our way to the village of Schönau, where in spring the meadows were golden with cowslips. At other times we went for a day out hiking. Summer holidays when I was small were spent on the Baltic coast, where the sand stretches for miles. This is known as the Amber Coast (*Bernsteinküste*), and my mother possessed an amber necklace which came from there. After the war a kind German friend sent it to me. One year, before my sister was born, we had a holiday at the Schliersee in the Alpine region south of Munich, not the high Alps but an area of lakes and lesser mountains. Every morning we found wild strawberries and raspberries for breakfast. Once, while we were out walking, a fierce thunderstorm raged above us: a truly frightening experience.

In later years my parents chose to spend holidays in the Rhön Mountains, first at a farmhouse on a hill called the Dreistelz. The farmer would meet us at the station with a cart pulled by a tractor. We also spent two holidays at the Kreuzberg in the Rhön, where there was a monastery with a guesthouse. Father always wanted to go hiking, and when I was old enough I joined him; sometimes the rest of the family came for shorter walks. One person who occasionally joined us for the day was Gustel Hess, a childhood friend of my father who later became a constant visitor to our family. She was unmarried and worked as a primary school teacher in Schweinfurt, north of Würzburg. She had an endless fund of stories, knew about wild flowers, and invented games for us children. Her collection of minerals inspired me, later, to collect unusual stones whenever I had the chance.

After the war I received many very moving letters from Gustel and other friends of my parents, Cilly Bodky and the Valetons, as well as others who wanted to commemorate my family:

From Gustel Hess

18 October 1947

My dear Hannah,

In the years when I could still visit your family at Keesburgstrasse in Würzburg, we always arranged an outing on the Sunday between your father's birthday (20 October) and mine (25 October). We walked somewhere or other, above the Main valley with its autumn scents, or through the brightly coloured woods near Gemünden, and celebrated everything that called for a celebration. Your father thought a blue sky dulled nature's colours. Only against a grey/white background would the colours really glow from inside. He sometimes became really ecstatic at seeing colours or lines in the landscape. And when I see such things, I feel he taught me to see, or helped me to see better.

In another letter (20 July 1947), Gustel relates that my parents helped to support the painter Josef Versl. He was and is well known in the region: born in 1901, he lived to be over 90. My father told Gustel with secret amusement that a painting by Versl which he owned had been shown at a national exhibition and bought by Hitler. In 1951, when my husband and I visited Versl, he himself told me this story, and insisted on presenting me with a framed watercolour of Würzburg because, he said, he owed it to my father.

Anna Valeton and her husband Professor Josué Valeton were close friends of my parents, and were among those who helped me to appreciate what kind of people they had been:

21 February 1947

Dear Hannah Weinberger,

.... Do you still remember how pretty and distinctive your mother always was in the clothes she wore? That she had a quite special style of her own? A very attractive mixture of a girl from the hiking club and a really great lady? In fact she was like that in her whole being.

And do you know that your father was the most respected and popular public prosecutor at the district court in Würzburg? That every defendant could consider himself lucky to have him as a prosecutor, since, just because he was a public prosecutor, he saw his main task in taking note of everything which could count in a defendant's favour? He once told me himself: "The task of the public prosecutor is not at all to accuse, but to prevent people who are harmless in themselves from getting into misfortune as a result of foolish and over-zealous charges."

My mother was very musical, and on our walks we sang folk-songs and rounds. She was a marvellous pianist and I particularly remember her playing Bach's Prelude and Fugue in C major from Book I of the *Well-Tempered Clavier*, Beethoven's Waldstein Sonata and Brahms' Variations and Fugue on a Theme by Handel. From a very early age I made up my own dances round the piano while she played. The Brahms Variations came at a time when I began to read the Greek stories of Odysseus and his travels, of Jason and the Golden Fleece. The long, spacious theme with its inner confidence became associated in my mind with heroic voyages into unknown regions. The child ignorant of composition technique nevertheless absorbed the variations as different moods and local colour; in the same way, each of the works my mother played regularly had for me its own atmosphere.

Mother occasionally played the violin as well. Every now and then she would invite friends in for an evening's singing: madrigals, rounds and church music. Sometimes she attended the services in Würzburg Cathedral, chiefly for the sake of the music. When I was eight, mother started to give me piano lessons. After some time she tried to arrange further lessons from an acquaintance who was a professional pianist. But this lady decided it would be dangerous for her career if it became known that she was teaching a Jewish child, so it did not happen.

My parents were not Orthodox Jews, and celebrated both the Jewish festival of Chanukah and Christmas. On Christmas Eve there was always great excitement. The children were not allowed into the sitting-room. For days there had been delicious smells wafting round the flat, as mother and our maid baked cinnamon, nut and spice cookies. Finally at six o'clock mother rang a silvery-toned bell and the door opened. There stood the tall Christmas tree with its candles alight; round it were ranged the presents, and for each member of the family a large plate heaped with cookies, nuts and mandarin oranges. But first we sang the traditional Christmas carols, and only then opened the presents.

Chanukah, the Jewish festival of lights, dates back to the second century BC. The Syrian king who had conquered Judea, as the Jewish state was then called, wanted to abolish the Jewish religion. But the Jews, under their leader Judas Maccabeus, fought back, and in 164 BC the temple in Jerusalem was rededicated. Although only enough sanctified oil could be found to light the menorah, the branched candlestick in the temple, for one day, by a miracle this oil lasted for eight days. To commemorate this miracle, Jews light an eight-branched menorah in their homes, starting with one light, until on the final evening all eight are burning. While the menorah is alight, the members of the family sing, tell stories or play games.

One spring I was staying with my Weinberger grandparents in Bayreuth and celebrated Passover with them. This great festival commemorates the flight of the Jews, led by Moses, from slavery in Egypt. It is celebrated at about the same time as Easter. The festival lasts for eight days, and the most important part of it is the Seder meal on the first evening. Special foods are eaten: matzah, i.e. bread made without yeast, reminds everyone that the children of Israel had to flee from Egypt in haste, so they could not wait for the dough to rise. Other foods include parsley or celery, dipped in salt water: these signify the fruits of the earth. Horseradish, and the salt water, symbolize the bitterness of slavery. A sweet dish consists of a mixture of nuts, almonds, apples, spices and wine. A roast lamb bone and a boiled egg recall sacrifices in the temple at Jerusalem. Blessings are said over each course, and wine is drunk at certain stages. Early in the Seder meal the youngest child present asks four questions; in reply the father tells the story of the flight from Egypt.

After my sister was born in 1936, my parents decided that with three children they needed a bigger flat. Therefore in June, we moved to a spacious apartment in a private house at Keesburgstrasse, built for three families. We lived on the ground floor; the owner, Herr Bauer and his family, on the first, and someone else at the top of the house. On moving day, Mother told me to walk straight from school to the new address. At that time my school was timetabled for a long morning, 8.00 a.m. to 1.30 p.m.; the afternoon was free. So I made my way to the new house expecting to see my family, and the removal van being unloaded. No one! Nothing! Even for an eight-year-old proud of being the eldest, this quickly led to a feeling of being abandoned. But as soon as I rang the bell of the Bauers' flat, Frau Bauer sized up the situation and took me in to share their lunch. When my family did arrive during the afternoon, she welcomed them with a huge bunch of lilac blossom from the garden. Her generosity was followed by many other acts of kindness by the Bauer family, and even now, when the lilac is in flower, its scent invariably recalls that day.

* * *

My first three years at school were spent at a large state primary school in the centre of Würzburg. I used to walk with my father to the public law office where he worked; then I continued to school across the parade ground in front of the extensive and splendid bishop's palace known as the *Residenz*. Until 1871, Würzburg had been a separate state where the bishop was also the temporal ruler. The *Residenz* was built in the eighteenth century to rival the French palace of Versailles. The ceiling of its magnificent staircase is decorated with marvellous frescoes by the Italian painter Tiepolo.

During my three years at the primary school, there was one occasion when all the pupils had to parade in the courtyard to listen to a speech by the Nazi minister Hermann Goering, and give the 'Heil Hitler' salute. What I chiefly remember is the boredom of waiting for hours in the courtyard, and, on seeing Goering, my astonishment that anyone could be so fat.

Another memory linked with this school concerns the bus stop where I waited on wet days for the bus home. On the wall nearby was a glass case in which was displayed a notorious anti-semitic propaganda sheet called *Der Stürmer (The Stormtrooper)*. This was edited by a Bavarian Nazi called Julius Streicher, and each new edition featured degrading caricatures of Jewish faces on the front page. It formed a part of the ceaseless hate campaign against the Jews, masterminded by Joseph Goebbels, Hitler's minister of propaganda.

As soon as Hitler and his ministers came to power in 1933, they began to carry out the reorganization of the German state along clearly defined lines. The changes were known collectively as *Gleichschaltung* (co-ordination). Anyone opposing these measures had to reckon with violent reprisals by the Secret State Police (Gestapo), set up by Goering in 1933. Some of the main areas affected were: a) the abolition of all political parties and of democracy, b) the creation of a single, centralized German state in place of the federal system of *Länder* (states such as Bavaria within the larger country), and c) the break-up of the trade unions and confiscation of their funds. Members of the civil service who did not support the Nazi ideology or could not prove that their families were of pure Aryan (non-Jewish) race, lost their jobs.

At a special meeting of the Reichstag in Nuremberg in 1935, the Nuremberg Laws were passed. These deprived German Jews of citizenship and forbade intermarriage of Jews with Germans. This meant for example that my cousin Hanna Jacobsohn, who was half-Jewish, could not marry her fiancé Walter Naumann, who was 'pure' German. The only way they could marry was by emigrating under great difficulties to the USA. The anti-Jewish views of Hitler and his ministers, proclaimed well before they came to power, were put into practice as soon as they took over the government. To them the Jews were the scapegoats, responsible for defeat after World War I, for the chaotic inflation and the massive unemployment. Nothing was allowed to stand in the way of eliminating them from positions in the state, of persecuting them and finally destroying them.

As a result of the law for 'purifying' the civil service, many Jewish professionals including university teachers were dismissed. When my uncle Hermann Jacobsohn was informed in March 1933 that he could not continue his work as a professor in Marburg, he committed suicide by throwing himself in front of a train. His four children were also affected by the punitive race laws. The youngest son, Adolf, was sent by his mother to a boarding school in England. The two daughters, Lore and Hanna, had to give up their university studies and later emigrated. Only the eldest son, Helmuth, was able to stay in Germany with his widowed non-Jewish mother.

My father on the other hand was not dismissed immediately from his post in the state law service. As he had fought for Germany in the First World War and had also been wounded, the Nazis allowed him to continue until (I think) 1937, when he was forced to 'retire' at the age of 48. During this period my mother was kept busy looking after my brother and my little sister, and working in her garden. So, after school and at weekends, my father would take me for long walks through the vineyards not far from our home on the edge of town. He never said anything about the political situation, but answered the questions I was asking, like a lot of nine-year-olds, about the sun, the moon and the tides, strange places, strange peoples, animals and so on. At the turning point of our walks we usually visited a little café in the village of Heidingsfeld, where they served a special kind of chocolate cake filled with whipped cream. I learnt so much during these walks, and I like to think that my father found some comfort, some compensation for the loss of his career in guiding the mind of a lively child.

After my Jacobsohn grandmother in Lüneburg died in 1934, my mother probably inherited some money with which she bought a large garden near the vineyards, within walking distance of our home. The garden was well stocked with plum and other fruit trees, with black, red and white currant bushes, gooseberries and other produce. Mother did the garden work herself and was happy to grow fresh fruit and vegetables for the family. At a deeper level, she must have been helped by all this activity in the garden to forget the increasingly threatening situation, if only for an hour at a time.

After three years at the state primary school, I was forced to leave in (I think) 1937. It was said that the presence of Jewish children polluted the atmosphere for the German children of 'pure Aryan' descent. From then on I attended the Jewish school just across the courtyard from the synagogue, in one of the narrow streets in the centre of Würzburg. We were taught elementary Hebrew in addition to normal school subjects, as many families hoped to emigrate to Palestine, as Israel was then called. Later we were also given a crash course in English by an excellent woman teacher, since more and more families were emigrating to English-speaking countries. This one-year course was so effective that when I arrived in England in 1939, I was able to understand quite a lot of what was said to me and to communicate in my turn, if only at a simple level.

One incident, probably in 1938, brought home to me that even a child could unwittingly place the family in danger. I had been given a scooter, and later, some roller-skates. Playing with another girl, I had the stupid idea of riding the scooter while still wearing the roller skates: showing off, in fact. Inevitably I fell off, falling into the road straight in front of a bus. Fortunately the driver managed to brake in time. Very shocked, he demanded to see my parents, who were later visited by a bus inspector and the police. My parents, greatly relieved that I was not hurt, did not punish me as I deserved. They clearly thought I would in future avoid anything that would attract official attention. I felt very ashamed to have caused them distress as a result of my childish thoughtlessness. Unfortunately, within a few months *all* Jews were to experience persecution on a national scale, for no other reason than that they were Jews.

Chapter Three

Kristallnacht, November 1938 – My First Months in England – My Family in Wartime

From 1933 onwards, Jews had been leaving Germany. My cousin Fritz Levinger gave up his law studies on the day Hitler came to power, and emigrated to Palestine; his parents followed as soon as they could. Later my aunt Martha Meyer and her family went to Holland. My cousin Lore Jacobsohn went to Switzerland. My uncle Leo Weinberger could no longer practise as a solicitor from January 1938. He and his wife Lisel and his brother Max emigrated in 1938 to California, USA.

Why did my father not take steps at that time to arrange our family's emigration? Friends wrote to me after the war that at first he could not imagine leaving all that was good in Germany and bringing up his children in a foreign country. He had fought for Germany in the First World War and had worked loyally for the German state legal service without feeling in any way different from those around him. Moreover, the strict immigration rules for Britain and the USA required that immigrants must prove their ability to earn their own living or show a firm promise of support from someone in the host country. After the widespread unemployment of the early 1930s, these countries were not prepared to admit people who might become a burden on the state. My father could see no way of working as a lawyer in another country without taking all his examinations again, which was out of the question. My uncles in California managed to make some sort of a living by setting up a small business selling materials for shoe repairs. But my father, almost fifty, had no training in business and would not have been able to do this.

In November 1938 an event occurred that brought things to a head. Herschel Grynszpan, a young Jew of Polish origin in Paris, in despair at the Nazis' brutal treatment of his parents, shot and killed a German diplomat. Immediately the Nazis ordered attacks throughout Germany on Jewish homes, synagogues and shops.This night, November 9-10, became known as *Kristallnacht*, or Night of Broken Glass, because the streets in all the towns and cities were filled with shattered glass. Almost 100 Jews were killed, and approximately 30,000 Jewish men were sent to concentration camps.

On that night my father was away in northern Germany, dealing with matters connected with the house of my Jacobsohn grandparents in Lüneburg. My mother was in the flat with us three children and our maid. Suddenly a loud hammering was heard on the outer door. Herr Bauer and his elder son valiantly tried to protect us, but were overwhelmed by four or five thugs who burst into our flat. We were herded into the kitchen and not physically harmed. However, my mother's china and glass cabinet was smashed to pieces, and so was her glass-fronted linen cupboard, on top of which stood rows of preserving jars filled with plums from the garden. The clean white sheets stained with red plum juice will always remain in my memory.

The tension and anxiety of the days following *Kristallnacht* is shown in two letters my father wrote to Gustel Hess. The first is postmarked Hanover, 14 November 1938:

Monday

Dear Gustel

I thank you from the bottom of my heart [for a letter]. In the end I did not know whether I should return for Ruth's sake or ought to stay away. Now Ruth has heard nothing from me since the telephone conversation on Friday evening [11 November], but she knew I would be here on Sunday... I hope, from your letter, that you will meet Ruth on Wednesday...

The rest of this letter reports on meetings with relatives and others, and states that he proposes to visit Cousin Hanna next day, to discuss inheritance business. But a short note postmarked the next day says simply: "I am just about to return home! Because Ruth wishes it. Warmest greetings. K."

Note that no signature or address are included in these letters, for fear of being identified by the Nazi censorship.

The fathers of several of my schoolmates were taken to concentration camps immediately after *Kristallnacht*. We were thankful that my father was not; he must have begun at once to start planning for our emigration. My uncles in the USA were willing to give the required guarantees for initial support of the family. But since tens of thousands of Jews were also trying to emigrate, there were long queues and delays of many months.

The violence done during *Kristallnacht* to parts of our flat was only one instance of the widespread attacks on Jewish property throughout Germany. In Würzburg the synagogue was destroyed, candlesticks and articles used in the religious service were broken. The Torah scrolls, rolled-up parchments on which the five books of Moses in the Old Testament are inscribed by hand, and which are venerated as the word of God, were burnt. The Jewish school across the courtyard was also destroyed. When we returned to school, we found the furniture broken, with books and other articles strewn around in disorder. I was particularly upset about my needlework project: it was to have been a short apron, and Mother had taken me into town on a special trip to choose the apple-green linen with pink and brown embroidery thread. It did not survive the attack. From now on we had classes in one of the few remaining Jewish buildings with a large enough room. It was like a village school in which lessons for different age groups were held simultaneously. During the time until I left the following June, the number of children fell steadily as more and more families emigrated.

Why did the Western Allies, who had had responsibility for carrying out the provisions of the Versailles Treaty in the 1920s, not intervene to stop Hitler in the 1930s? Western governments were frightened of Communism, which had taken over in Russia, a cruel and dictatorial regime under Stalin. They were afraid, especially after the worldwide economic depression from 1929 to the early 1930s, that the growing Socialist parties in their own countries might bring about a Communist revolution there. So, watching Hitler's swift moves against German Socialists after he came to power, they regarded him as an ally. They chose not to understand the increasing cruelty of his policies against the Jews, although they were told about them by reliable witnesses. Some historians believe that if they had expressed their disapproval firmly, instead of appeasing Hitler, he would not have dared to persecute the Jews so cruelly and so comprehensively.

* * *

Miss Nell Gill, a teacher in Bristol, had been concerned about the persecution of the Jews in Germany. She belonged to the Fellowship of Reconciliation, a Christian association working for peace. Through this group, she and the colleague who shared her flat were given the name of my cousin Hanna, and decided to offer her a holiday in England, about 1934 or 1935. Hanna stayed about three months, improving her English but also giving German conversation lessons and talking with senior pupils.

Later my cousin worked elsewhere in England, keeping up the friendship with Nell. When Hanna's fiancé Walter moved to the USA, Nell offered to let Hanna stay with her until marriage in the USA was possible. But my cousin preferred to stay with her widowed mother in Marburg as long as she could. Nell then suggested that I should come, as Hanna had told her that Jewish children were only allowed to attend school until the age of eleven. So my cousin gave up her chance of leaving Nazi Germany for me. Fortunately, being only half-Jewish, she later managed to leave Germany after the war had started, sailing to the USA from Portugal in December 1940, a journey of eleven days.

Nell came to visit our family in Würzburg at Easter 1939, so when my parents applied to the Quakers to have me sent to England on a special children's train (*Kindertransport*), they knew I would be going to a friend. As well as travel tickets, my parents had to obtain a passport for me. The official papers concerning this request still exist in the State Archives in Würzburg, and were copied for me by Professor Hans-Joachim Vollrath. The application had to be approved by the Secret State Police (*Geheime Staatspolizei* or *Gestapo*). The fifth sheet (out of nine), see pp. 48-49, bears the heading:

> Letter to Police Headquarters: Passport Office, sent on 18 April 1939
>
> Concerns: Preparatory measures to changing one's domicile to a foreign country
>
> There are no political objections to issuing a passport for the purpose of attending school in England, and later emigrating to the USA, for the Jewish person Hanna Gertrud Sara Weinberger, born on 3.2.1928 at Hof on the Saale, living at Würzburg, Keesburgstrasse 20. Signed ...

Akten

der

Geheimen Staatspolizei

Staatspolizeistelle

Würzburg

über

Weinberger Hanna, ~~[illegible]~~

(Familien- und Vornamen)

3. 2. 1920

(Geburtsdatum)

Hof a/S.

(Geburtsort)

Akz.

Staatsarchiv Würzburg
Gestapostelle Würzburg

16848

Application to the Gestapo for a Passport,
Staatsarchiv, Würzburg; File: Gestapo 16848

(with permission of the Staatsarchiv)

Kanzlei
erhalten am: 17. IV. 39
gefertigt: 18.4.39.
gelesen: 18. IV. 39
abgesandt: 18. IV. 39

Nr. II B.

I. Kanzlei : Schreiben an

die Polizeidirektion - Paßstelle -

Würzburg.

Betreff : Vorbereitende Maßnahmen zur Verlegung des Wohnsitzes ins Ausland.

Bezug : Dort. Schreiben v. 6.4.1939, Nr. 3239.

Gegen die Ausstellung eines Passes zum Schulbesuch in England und zur späteren Auswanderung für die Jüdin Hanna Gertrud Sara Weinberger, geb. am 3.2.1928 zu Hof.a.S., wohnhaft in Würzburg, Keesburgstraße 2o, bestehen politisch keine Bedenken.

II. Ausgewertet in der Kartei. Wa.

III. Weglegen als Pers. Akt: Weinberger Hanna Gertrud Sara.

Würzburg, den 14. April 1939.
Geheime Staatspolizei
Staatspolizeistelle
I. A.

Wa.

Application to the Gestapo for a Passport: Letter to Police Headquarters; Staatsarchiv, Würzburg; File: Gestapo 16848

(with permission of the Staatsarchiv)

The Weinberger children, 1939; left to right: Hannah, Lies and Micheli, and back cover

Nell Gill, with Lies, Würzburg, 1939

Nell Gill and her parents, Alice and Horace, during the Second World War

Aunt Grete Jacobsohn in Marburg, in the 1940s

Hannah at Redland High School, Bristol, in 1944
(back row, second from left)

Deutsches Rotes Kreuz
Präsidium / Auslandsdienst
Berlin SW 61, Blücherplatz 2

23. JUN 1943 - 543537

ANTRAG
an die *Agence Centrale des Prisonniers de Guerre, Genf*
— Internationales Komitee vom Roten Kreuz —
auf Nachrichtenvermittlung

REQUÊTE
de la Croix-Rouge Allemande, Présidence, Service Etranger
à l'Agence Centrale des Prisonniers de Guerre, Genève
— Comité International de la Croix-Rouge —
concernant la correspondance

1. Absender / *Expéditeur*: Ruth Sara Weinberger. Würzburg, Bibrastrasse 6.

bittet, an
prie de bien vouloir faire parvenir à

2. Empfänger / *Destinataire*: Hanna Weinberger. Bristol/England 12 The Paragon

folgendes zu übermitteln / *ce qui suit:*

(Höchstzahl 25 Worte!)
(25 mots au plus!)

Grosse Freude über Deine Aprilnachricht! Verlegen morgen unseren Wohnsitz nach Osten. Sind guten Mutes. Alle gesund. Schreib Tante Grete. Innige Grüsse

Würzburg, 16. Juni 1943

(Datum / date)

Mutter

(Unterschrift / Signature)

COMITÉ INTERNATIONAL DE LA CROIX-ROUGE GENÈVE

3. Empfänger antwortet umseitig
Destinataire répond au verso

Michael

Last Red Cross letter from my mother, dated 16 June 1943, and front cover

Hannah Weinberger and Aubrey Hickman, Cheddar, 1948

Aubrey Hickman, Manchester, 1970s.
Photo taken by Mark Hansel.

Hannah Hickman, 2001

The seventh sheet, dated 1943, refers to a sum of money which my parents had deposited in my name with the Hamburg-Amerika Shipping Company. The document declares that according to a law passed in 1941, money belonging to Jews who have emigrated is to become the property of the German state. It also says that according to this law I have lost German nationality. A copy of the relevant section of the law was kindly made for me by Dr Hans-Peter Baum of the Jewish Documentation Centre in Würzburg. Professor Vollrath, when he sent me the emigration papers in 1996, commented on how depressing he found it that in the Nazi state, injustice was administered according to the correct bureaucratic procedures. "Perhaps, in many cases, this prevented an awareness of the injustice which one would really expect." He also blamed the German education system of the time. For generations German schools had regarded obedience to authority as the highest virtue; Hitler's proclamation of himself as supreme leader reinforced this even more. By contrast, Herr Vollrath quoted from the great Rabbi Leo Baeck, who wrote about what it means to be Jewish. He stated that unless people were prepared to take independent decisions, they would be unable to act according to moral laws.

My journey to England is described in the Introduction to this book. It must have been very hard for my parents to let me go into an unknown future, though not to an unknown home. By then, the situation had become so desperate that they must have accepted Nell's offer of asylum for me with relief and gratitude. At that stage, they still hoped to emigrate themselves, so that we could all be reunited. Another English friend of my cousin, Dr Dorothy Emmet, offered to care for my brother and sister. A date was fixed and a friend went to Tilbury Docks to meet the ship. But at the last moment, Mother sent a cable that the children were not coming. In the summer of 1939 Michael was seven and Elisabeth was three. My parents must have felt that the children were too young to face exile on their own.

When I arrived in Bristol on 6 June 1939, Nell took me to her flat. It was at 12 The Paragon in Clifton, one of several early nineteenth-century crescents near the Clifton Suspension Bridge. The house belonged to Mr and Mrs Green, who were very kind to me. Sometimes on a Sunday they invited Nell and me to go out in their car to have a picnic on the Mendip Hills south of Bristol. On at least one occasion, once the war had started, we all joined in building small pyramids of turf on top of a long, flat hill. These were about two metres high and were intended to prevent German aircraft from landing.

Nell was head of the mathematics department at Redland High School in Bristol. The school is in a beautiful eighteenth-century building with a large garden, and I attended the school from the time I arrived. It was then a fee-paying school, and Nell paid for me during the first two months and the following year. Then the governors gave me a scholarship for the fees. Many people helped me in all sorts of ways. The school secretary, Miss Shaw, paid for my lunches. The piano teacher, Miss Cove, gave me free piano lessons throughout my time at the school, a fact I only discovered after I had left. Her kindness was of vital importance to me in keeping alive the involvement with music I had brought from home. I enjoyed the piano and later passed Grade VII of the Associated Board examinations. Fortunately, at a later stage I was able to repay some of her generosity. Miss Berwick, the headmistress during my first years, paid for me to have cello lessons. The teacher, Miss Pullen, was an old lady with tight white curls. In her younger days she had played in cinemas with a violinist and a pianist, providing music for silent films.

Nell's parents, sisters and brother all accepted me as part of the family and invited me to stay at Christmas and other holidays. The parents of my fellow pupils were also very helpful. One, Mrs Webb, lent me her daughter's books. I raced through volumes of *Anne of Green Gables* and *What Katy Did*, which did wonders for my fluency in English. Mr and Mrs Jones, parents of my schoolmate Sheila, invited me to stay for weekends when Nell was taking older girls walking in the Cotswold Hills.

The activities of the Bristol Council for Refugees, under its director Mrs Falk, ensured that I and other child refugees were recognized as victims of the Nazi regime and not treated as enemy aliens. I was very fortunate to encounter only kindness and encouragement. Some young refugees, only a little older than myself, were offered accommodation in England and then treated as servants by the host families. In my case, not only the adults but also fellow pupils accepted me with good will. The one exception, once the war had begun, was a girl sitting behind me in class who tried to stick drawing pins into my back, chanting "Britons never, never, never shall be slaves." The teacher soon put a stop to that.

In the three months from my arrival until the start of war on 3 September 1939, my parents and Weinberger grandparents wrote to me constantly, and I to them. After this, letters were forwarded by my aunt in Holland, until that country was overrun by the German army in 1940. The letters written to me after that must have come via cousin Lore in Switzerland or the relations in the USA. Those dated 1940 are marked with a number by a censor. After this there are no normal letters to me, but messages and family news via Switzerland and the USA, until the USA entered the war against Germany in December 1941, bringing the postal service between these two countries to a halt.

Here is a letter from my mother:

6 August 1939

My dear Hannah,

I am quite sad that I haven't written to you for so long, tomorrow it will be two weeks probably, or longer? And you have been writing so steadily, many thanks; we are very pleased that you are having such a good time on Dartmoor. Your two cards are really beautiful, and we just looked at the atlas to find out where you are now. There are surely many beautiful and interesting things to see there. And I hope you continue to have good weather. We are just having a very long and at first very severe thunderstorm, even though today started rather cool. We are now very busy with fruit, peaches are ripe and small pears, two trees next to your 'bathing tub'; they taste very good but also rot quickly. Grandfather enjoyed the garden very much and eagerly helped to collect pears and pick gooseberries. For Lies [my sister] if it is warm, I put out the small bath to splash around in, and she likes the cold water. Micheli [my brother] built himself a small tent next to the sandpit at the start of the holidays. The flowers you sowed are flowering well, and even a few cyclamen in the rock garden. So far I didn't tell you that Gretel [our former maid] visited us the other day! That was very nice. She is tall and slim and asked about everyone, of course specially about you, too, and was pleased that 'big' Hanna was there, and almost felt insulted because Micheli didn't recognize her at once.

And now we must thank you for your school report and for the photos! Of course we are delighted with all of them! The report is very good for a start, and in gymnastics you haven't had as much practice as the others, that will come later. It's very good that Edith [another refugee] and you will now go into the Main School. The photos of Commemoration Day are beautiful. And you sent us a very nice description of your normal day. I typed a copy of your letter about your journey for Aunt Lisel, she was so keen to have more news of you. Have you written to her now in the holidays? Have you had a letter from her yet? Has Micheli written to you? He seems to like it there with Hanna [in Marburg]. Marianne [a Würzburg friend] sent this letter for you.

I am glad that you are allowed to go to the cinema, I only wrote that comment the other day because of the frightening film. Please tell Nell that I am not worried about it, and many thanks for her letter, I'll write to her soon! From Dorothy we have quite good news, and hope things will continue so well. It is a pity you cannot go to Norfolk, especially for Nell! On the 2nd the Valentins left [cousins from Hamburg]; they are going to Croydon near London. Do write to them from London;

perhaps you can see them or meet them somewhere, if your travel money is sufficient – but only if you would like to, and have time.

Please give our warm greetings to Mrs Gill and the whole family, especially Connie and Nell!

A kiss for you from your Mummy.

During the summer holidays in 1939, Nell and I were invited to a cottage on Dartmoor by Miss St John and Miss Andrews, teachers at Redland High School. The heather reminded me of the Lüneburg Heath, but the rock formations known as tors were very strange. We then visited Nell's parents in Leytonstone, London. Nell's sister Connie started giving me pocket money every month and kept this up throughout my school years. Finally we visited Cornwall with Connie and a friend. The cliffs and sometimes crashing waves were exciting, very different from the calm seas of the Baltic I had known as a young child. The food was different, too, and I especially liked the scones with jam and clotted cream!

At the start of the war we were all given gas masks, to be carried at all times. Food was rationed, blackout was imposed at night. Bristol did not experience bombing at first. Nell's younger brother Bill joined the army. For the children at Redland, the main focus of attention was still our school work, and I was fortunate to have music lessons as well.

* * *

My uncles in California continued their efforts to get my family out of Germany, first to England and then to the USA. Later Uncle Leo gave this account to Professor Valeton:

Los Angeles, 1 September 1946

Dear Professor Valeton,

In 1939, at the time Hannah came to England, we had succeeded in obtaining all the necessary guarantees for the move of the whole family to England. The first delay occurred as the result of a misunderstanding by the consul in Bristol, to whom we had sent the papers as instructed. The consul had sent these papers on to Stuttgart [the American consulate]. The new papers which we acquired at once had arrived just in time. Then the immigration was delayed once more because, as we heard later, dear Ruth wanted to wait for a work permit for England before emigrating. Before this came through, the war broke out and all our hopes were dashed. In 1941 there was a small glimmer of hope, the possibility of emigrating to Cuba. Only very few people were able to escape this way at that time. The costs of this enterprise had by now become huge, and in view of the number of our family members [including the Weinberger grandparents], very much higher than our very limited resources. Nevertheless, we tried then, too, to make all the necessary arrangements, but the scheme was already stopped before we were able to complete our efforts.

Hoping to hear from you direct and soon, we remain with best wishes for you and your wife,

Leo Weinberger

My parents' letters to me do not mention the great anxiety they must have felt about the chances of emigrating, except for the veiled reference to Dorothy Emmet's plans for my brother and sister in the letter of 6 August 1939. Life for the Jews remaining in Germany became more and more restricted. From November 1938 they were forbidden to run shops or workshops. Their driving licences were confiscated in December 1938. After the death of the German diplomat which led to *Kristallnacht*, a payment of a thousand million Reichsmarks was imposed as a punishment on the whole Jewish community in Germany. I clearly remember my mother sorting out gold and silver articles to be handed in, and assume it must have been then. Out of the silver cutlery set which had come from Lüneburg, we were only allowed to keep one knife, fork and spoon for each member of the family.

In late 1938 the Nazi authorities began the process of removing Jews from their flats or houses, and collecting them into so-called Jews' houses. I do not know if my family's move in October 1939 to a smaller flat in Hofmeierstrasse was forced upon them or not, but it seems probable. From the start of the war in September 1939, Jews had to stay indoors in winter from 8.00 p.m., in summer from 9.00 p.m. My young brother Micheli, aged eight, experienced such restrictions at first hand. At one point a ruling came into force stating that Jewish children could not play outside. Cousin Lore remembered in 1995 that he was sent to stay with Cousin Hanna in Marburg, who told him: "Here you can play with the children in the street, they don't know you are Jewish." After a few days he himself told them he *was* Jewish, then he could no longer play outside. Then their parents came to Hanna and her mother, saying: "If you don't send him away, we'll smash your windows in." So he had to go back to Würzburg, where he could not play outside anyway.

It is almost impossible to believe the hysteria that had taken hold of the German people, even to the extent of forbidding children to play in the street. The fanatical hatred of the Jews, preached by Hitler, spread by Goebbels and his propaganda machine, gradually took hold of ordinary people and led them into crimes justified, in their eyes, by the goal of building up a 'purified' German nation. With some honourable exceptions, they were unable to see that their actions produced a state that was criminal in all its actions, the very opposite of 'pure'.

From autumn 1941 all Jews over six years old had to wear a yellow six-pointed Star of David, so that they could always be recognized as Jews. Bicycles, typewriters, cameras and binoculars had to be handed in. After 15 November 1938, Jewish children could no longer attend state schools; on 30 June 1942, private Jewish schools were closed as well.

Herr Bauer, who with his son had bravely tried to protect us on *Kristallnacht*, was punished by the Nazis for his courage. He had never been a member of the Nazi party, but had belonged since 1935 to the National Socialist People's Welfare organization (NSV), in which he served as local leader of a block of houses. He took it to be simply a welfare association, without realizing that after a few years the party connection became more important than its original stated purpose. His daughter Anneliese wrote to me in January 1948 that after his intervention on our behalf, he had been thrown out of the NSV in a full assembly, his house had been searched, and from then on party officials had regarded him as untrustworthy.

My father, who had previously distanced himself from the Jewish religion, was asked some time after I had emigrated if he would consider serving as the civic head of the Jewish community in Würzburg. There were very few people left who could take on this task, and he had always been regarded with the greatest respect. He agreed to serve, and Anna Valeton told me, in a letter on 21 July 1947, that my father then conscientiously observed the laws of the Jewish religion in order to be united with the people among whom he lived. In an earlier letter (5 October 1946, the first she sent me after the war), she wrote that my father told her he had long had doubts about his profession as public prosecutor, and that his work in the community fulfilled him as nothing had done before. Here is part of a letter from Gustel Hess to my Uncle Leo in the USA after the war (probably 1946):

Dear Herr Weinberger,

When I visited Karl and Ruth [in the most difficult years] I only heard a little of the good that Karl, as the leader and adviser of the Jewish community, was doing for the people suffering sorrow and fear, and how with his sense of justice he found the right way between the demands of humanity and those of the Third Reich. The police officials, especially, held him in high regard. People often reported highlights to me. Karl, this truly good and clear-minded man, judged and resolved matters with his deep, selfless understanding.

At this period, 1939, '40, '41, there was often the risk that these four people would have to leave the cramped flat in Herr Siegel's house, the beautiful garden there, and to leave all furniture behind. Yet they did not live in fear of such orders, but found a way of really taking leave in their minds of all these things, and thankfully accepting all that was left as a gift. Once, when I visited, Karl said, "I have now accepted all external losses, have separated myself from everything, I am inwardly free of all that. That produces a wonderful state of floating above things."

The Franconian landscape became one source of enrichment and joy for them both at that time. Schönau ... with its magnificent woods and the faithful people at the inn, the Kreuzberg with Pater Ratbert, intelligent and kind, the Dreistelz in the Rhön, they kept faith with these as long as was at all possible, finally walks in the Main valley and in the Guttenberg woods, which the children specially enjoyed. Ruth said once after Karl's death that this time of being together had been a climax for both of them. Micheli and Lies were purposefully kept ignorant of anything that might have oppressed the children, no conversation was allowed to touch on anything of that kind.

Warmest greetings from Gustel Hess

So my parents were able, in spite of increasing oppression, to live their lives with courage and inner peace, to care for the children and to help others where they could.

Chapter Four

The Start of War – My Grandparents and Other Relatives – My Father's Death in 1941 – My Life in Bristol up to 1942

The Second World War started in 1939 when Germany invaded Poland on 1 September. Britain had previously signed an alliance with Poland. On 3 September, Britain and France demanded an immediate promise of German withdrawal from Poland; since no reply was received, they declared war against Germany on that day.

History books give full details of the course of the war; here I can only mention a very few facts as a background to my story. At first things were relatively quiet to the west of Germany. Then in May 1940 the German army invaded Holland, conquering it in five days. They then moved against Belgium and northern France. Belgium capitulated, and a British force, as well as a large number of French soldiers, were saved in a dramatic rescue action from the port of Dunkirk. Paris was occupied and the French government signed an armistice with Germany.

From May 1940 Britain was ruled by a coalition government

under the Prime Minister, Winston Churchill, who had already held the chief post at the Admiralty in the First World War. Churchill was a man of great courage, experience and foresight. He was also a superb orator, and inspired the British will to resist Hitler by regular talks broadcast by the BBC.

After Britain had refused Hitler's peace offer, made in a speech on 19 July 1940, he planned to invade. But first he had to dispose of the Royal Air Force. From early August till late September 1940, the 'Battle of Britain' was at its height, with German bombers attacking ports, airfields and cities, but victory in the air was won by the courage and skill of the British fighter pilots. However, German bombers continued to attack Britain at night from September 1940 to May 1941.

In June 1941 Hitler invaded Russia, having long believed that the Germany of the future would need the living space of the Russian steppes. In the long run this invasion proved to be a costly failure, as a result of which millions of German and Russian troops, as well as civilians, died. Germany, with its ally Italy, also attacked in southern Europe, and in North Africa. The fact that Hitler was prepared to attack and risk German forces on so many fronts shows his megalomania, about which the professional officers of the German forces were becoming increasingly concerned. But since he had succeeded in establishing himself as Supreme Commander, they could do very little.

During all these years there was war at sea, with the Royal Navy escorting convoys of merchant ships bringing food across the Atlantic from the USA. On 7 December 1941, Japan attacked the American Pacific Fleet at Pearl Harbour, Hawaii. On 11 December 1941, Germany declared war against the USA, which now became Britain's strongest ally.

* * *

During my childhood and after I had left, my parents kept up a warm relationship with my paternal grandparents in Bayreuth, Josef and Rosette Weinberger. Once I stayed with them at Passover (see pp. 36-37). For their Golden Wedding meal in 1937, the table was set with a white damask tablecloth, silver cutlery and sparkling glasses. We had collected blue cornflowers from the fields and strewn them around the table for decoration. A roast goose was served, with a delicious taste.

The grandparents visited my family in Würzburg from time to time. On the occasion mentioned in Mother's letter of August 1939 (see page 59), Grandfather had come alone, either because Grandmother was not quite well, or because she wanted to look after her sister, Great-Aunt Helene. I only remember meeting this old lady once, in Bayreuth. My father had recently sent her an elegant umbrella for her birthday. On this particular day she had been invited to the house in Ludwigstrasse for afternoon coffee and cake. When the time came for her to go home, it started to rain. "But I can't walk home now!" she protested. "My new umbrella would get wet!" She gratefully accepted my father's offer to escort her, using *his* umbrella, and her saying was quoted with laughter to all our friends.

Great-Aunt Helene also sent me a birthday present around this time, which was very welcome. It was a fashionable lace-edged slip with matching panties in pale green, very different from the kind of underwear my mother usually provided. I was about eleven years old and felt very grown-up when I wore it.

My parents also continued their close relationship with Aunt Grete Jacobsohn in Marburg, the Gentile widow of my uncle Hermann, who had committed suicide when the Nazis came to power and dismissed him from his professorship. For several years she lived in the large family house with tenants in part of it. Her three younger children, Lore, Hanna and Adolf, were in exile. Her elder son, Helmuth, was for a time in the German army. She helped Jewish people where she could. The tenants wanted the house, but the Gestapo in Marburg were afraid to intervene because the family was so well known and respected in the city. The Gestapo in the nearby city of Kassel, however, put her in prison, although she had done nothing wrong and was over sixty.

One day the Gestapo wanted to take her away from prison to an unknown destination. The prison doctor told her to stay in bed. "But I'm not ill!" she said. Then some Polish girls who were also in the prison whispered to her what was likely to happen. She then accepted the pretence, and the prison doctor told the Gestapo she was too ill to be moved. A Professor of Theology told the Nazis that if they let her out, he would speak up for them when the tables were turned after the war, and she was allowed home.

Cousin Hanna, who told me about this in 1992, also explained what had happened to her brother Helmuth during the war. From 1939 he was called up to serve in the German army. He served in battle and was trained to defuse bombs. He was then recommended for officer training, since the military authorities were not anti-Jewish and wanted to treat everyone the same. But Hitler refused to allow half-Jews to become officers and ordered them to be dismissed from the army. On his return to Marburg, Helmuth was protected by Professor Hamann, a well known university professor, who insisted he needed Helmuth to assist in his research.

So it is clear that at least for half-Jews and their Gentile relatives, some brave Germans were prepared to stand up to the Nazis, even at risk to themselves.

* * *

In late 1941 my father became seriously ill and was taken to hospital in Würzburg. The exact nature of his illness is not entirely clear. Letters of the time speak of a blood disease. In earlier years, when we used to go hiking, he needed to bandage his legs, and sometimes rest for a day, and he explained that a wound he had suffered while fighting for Germany in the First World War, had left a piece of shrapnel embedded in his leg. So this may have been the cause of the blood infection. But beyond the immediate physical causes, there must have been a deep sadness in him at the systematic destruction of all he had lived for. His work as a lawyer for fairness and justice, his devotion to the good aspects of German culture, music, literature and art, his sense of belonging to a Germany he could respect and to the Jewish elements within it, all were denied by the brutality of Hitler's policies, willingly carried out by his followers.

My friend Anne (Anneliese) Hilb, ten years older than myself, also came to England before the war. Her parents were friends of my parents. Since she had relatives in Switzerland, a neutral country, they forwarded letters in wartime to and from her mother, Frau Marianne Hilb, until the mother and her elder daughter Irene were themselves deported to the death camp at Treblinka and murdered. At the time of my father's death, they were living in Frankfurt. Anne kindly gave me copies of letters from her mother, describing my father's suffering and how it affected the rest of my family:

15 December 1941

My dear Anneliese,

Today I have to tell you something infinitely more sad, that is, that fate has again snatched away one of the most splendid people from his family and from us. Only think, Herr Weinberger died a week ago tomorrow, on 9 December, as a result of blood poisoning, after being in bed 4-5 weeks with constant high fever, about three of these weeks in the hospital in Dürerstrasse. The only small consolation is ... that he himself was not truly aware of the gravity of his illness, but said, only a few days before his death, he must surely have been very seriously ill, and must now sleep a great deal. The last days he was unconscious, and then passed over into death quite peacefully at 5.30 am. Everything was done for him that could have been done. Certainly he could not have been treated more expertly anywhere else, all kinds of specialists were called in, but nothing could defeat the streptococci shown up by the blood analysis, and despite all drugs to stimulate the heart, it did not stand up to these demands. The cause of this blood poisoning probably lay in the disorder of the lymph glands of the one leg. However, for a long time the doctors did not realize this... I spoke to Ruth [my mother] on the telephone almost daily during this period – she had moved into the hospital with him – but even if we did not express our fears to one another, we knew that only a miracle could still save him. Unfortunately I could not visit ... , but at least I know that Ruth is surrounded by very many good loyal friends. In this last week too [since the death] I rang her several times and found her very calm and intent on helping her family to come to terms with it. Helmuth confirmed this for me on Saturday, on his return from W. [Würzburg] where he had stayed a few days after the funeral; he spent some hours here to tell me various details about the course of the illness. Karl's poor parents are now with Ruth. She would most like to take them to live with her, but does not know if it will be possible, it would indeed be the best solution for them all. The children of course were the first to accept the inevitable, but they show their full understanding by their lovable care and redoubled tenderness towards their mother. After Christmas, Helmuth's mother [Aunt Grete] will travel to Ruth and stay a while. What they intend to do about poor Hannah [myself in England] I do not know myself. Whether Lore [in Switzerland] will write and tell her, or whether they will keep her in ignorance. It was just possible to inform the brothers of the tragedy by telegram [i.e. my uncles in USA]. Helmuth said there had been immense expressions of sympathy in W. from all kinds of people, reflecting his popularity. One could say of K. W. [Karl Weinberger]... he had no enemies. In some ways it is good that I did not see him in his illness. He lives on in my mind as I saw him last in mid-September, looking a lot better than on his previous visit in June, with a good colour and fresh expression, reminding me of earlier, normal times. What will the Valentins say? and all other distant friends and relatives.

Finally I can assure you that we are all well.

With love and a special kiss for your birthday from your Mother.

Later, Frau Hilb wrote that it had, after all, *not* been possible to inform my uncles, presumably because the postal services from Germany to the USA were cut off from 11 December 1941, two days after my father died, when Germany declared war.

My father was buried in the Jewish cemetery on the road leading out of Würzburg in an easterly direction towards Nuremberg. The cemetery is still there, and the city of Würzburg has taken on the responsibility of maintaining it, with a warden who lives in an old house in the grounds. Gustel Hess generously looked after my father's grave and visited it regularly. After her death I was able to visit three times from England. I also arranged for a stonemason to carve the names of my mother, brother and sister, who have no known graves, on the headstone below my father's name.

* * *

My life with Nell Gill during World War II followed a pattern largely set by attendance at Redland High School in Bristol. Nell's flat at 12 The Paragon, Clifton, was some way from the school. At first we used to drive in her small Austin Seven car, but soon petrol was restricted to 'essential' users, so we cycled. Food was rationed and one had to present ration books in the shops, where the grocer or butcher cut out the coupons for the weekly allowance of butter, sugar, jam, bacon, meat etc., but school lunches were free of coupons, for which we were thankful!

Soon after the beginning of the new school year in September 1940, everyone at our school was shocked to hear that Barbara Vickery, the previous year's Head Girl, had been killed in a daylight air raid. She had been working at the Bristol Aeroplane Company factory at Filton near Bristol, before going to university, and was the victim of the first daylight air attack on Filton Aerodrome on 25 September. Even though most people at the school had relatives or friends directly involved in resisting Hitler, her death brought the war that much closer to us.

At night the streets were 'blacked out' so that enemy aircraft would not know where the city was. This meant no street lights, and black curtains or paper over the windows. Groups of volunteer air raid wardens were established in every street, to give help in case of air attack, with fire-fighting or in other ways. The Red Cross trained volunteers to give first aid to the injured. At Redland High School, the staff formed teams to act as wardens. There were not enough tin helmets to go round, so Nell tied an enamelled colander (strainer) over her head. One night when we were there, the attacking German planes dropped firebombs which split into smaller units, which then burst into flames. These fell on the flat roof of the school, an eighteenth-century building, whereupon several brave teachers picked them up and dropped them over the side into the garden.

At 12 The Paragon, whenever the air raid siren sounded, all the occupants took shelter. During the periods when air attacks were expected, I was usually allowed to sleep in the basement just below street level, in a room which had once been a kitchen. I could hear mice scrabbling in the old cupboards, which almost frightened me more than the prospect of attack! But when we heard the siren, we all went down one more level, to what had been the wine cellar of the old house, very solidly built with an arched stone ceiling. The Paragon is a crescent of houses dating from the Regency period at the beginning of the nineteenth century, standing at the top of a steep hill above the river Avon and the old harbour area. The river then flows between vertical cliffs under the Clifton Suspension Bridge. Down on the opposite shore, next to the harbour, are some large factory buildings, and behind them the land gradually rises up to Bedminster Down. One night, I remember, the German bombers were approaching from that direction. We clearly heard bombs explode beyond the river, then in the harbour valley. Judging by the time interval between these two, I was convinced that the next one would hit us. What a relief when we heard it explode on the other side! In this and other raids, parts of the Clifton shopping area and large areas of the city centre were very badly damaged and many people killed.

At the beginning of the war the Nazi leaders had boasted that it would all be over in a flash, a *Blitzkrieg* (lightning war). In fact it lasted six years, but the name stuck. So, talking about the bombing attacks aimed at various cities, sometimes for months on end, people spoke of the London Blitz, the Bristol Blitz, and so on. The Western Allies were bombing German cities at the same time, two of the most severe attacks being those on Hamburg and Dresden. In March 1945 American ground forces were advancing on Würzburg, and their commander offered to spare this historic city by declaring it to be a hospital zone. But the local *Gauleiter* (regional leader), a rabid Nazi, refused to surrender. Therefore the British Royal Air Force was ordered to strike, and in one night, 16 March 1945, the city was almost totally destroyed, less than two months before the end of the war. My parents' loyal friends fortunately survived, but all lost their homes.

We were encouraged to learn to recognize the silhouettes of British and German aircraft. Two British fighter planes, the Spitfire and the Hurricane, became especially famous for their exploits and the bravery of their pilots. Once, on a sunny morning, we in The Paragon watched from the terrace as a Hurricane and a German fighter, probably a Messerschmitt, fought an air duel in the clear blue sky beyond the river. The German plane was shot down and fell slowly to earth, followed by a spiral of black smoke. This was the only military action I witnessed myself. Aubrey Hickman, whom I met in 1946 and later married, had served in the Royal Navy and had some dramatic stories to tell about his war years.

* * *

From the time I started on the first full year at the school in September 1939, I worked hard. Although only eleven years old, I was very aware of the kindness shown to me by Nell and so many others, and determined to prove myself worthy of it. At first I was placed in a class whose average age was a little lower than mine, so that I would find the school work easier and have more chance to perfect my English. Before Easter 1940, the teachers decided that by the autumn I would be ready to skip the next class and join the one above. It was at this time that the first period of bombing started in Bristol. Nell's sister, Connie, had been evacuated with the London school where she taught to the safety of Dulverton, a village in Somerset. So for some weeks in the summer holidays I lived there in a small hotel, with Connie in charge. I had no classes, but school work still had to be done, and most of all the beginnings of Latin, for the class I was to join would already have started this. There I sat in the hot sun, on a bench by the little river in Dulverton, reciting *Mensa, mensa, mensam* and all the other noun, verb and adjective tables in Kennedy's *Shorter Latin Primer*. It must have worked, for I was then able to move to the older class without difficulty.

I was truly fortunate to attend this school, founded in 1882 with the express purpose of giving higher education to girls. The principle underlying all its activities was to allow every girl to develop her full potential, whether academic, practical or artistic, or a combination of all three. Each year had an academic stream aiming at university, and a more practical stream aiming perhaps at teacher training college or nursing. Looking back, it does not seem to me that the anxieties and problems of war prevented any of the teachers from giving their best and expecting it of the pupils.

In spring 1942 news came to the school that my father had died the previous December. As far as I recall, it was the headmistress who told me, very gently, suggesting that I might like to miss the rest of my lessons and walk home. I left the school and walked along The Downs, an extensive natural park above the Avon cliffs. Sitting under a clump of trees, I cried a little as I realized that I would never see my father again. For the first time I began to understand that I might indeed never see any of my family again. By this time I was fourteen years old, and suddenly made to face aspects of my situation that had been hidden up to now behind everyday concerns. But at the house, Mr and Mrs Green, and Nell in the evening, helped me to come to terms with my loss. In the next holiday period, Miss Jones, my French teacher, invited Nell and me to stay in her small chalet at Saundersfoot on the South Pembrokeshire coast, a typical act of generosity.

By now I was already preparing for public examinations, and later moved into the senior part of the school, taking on some responsibilities. There will be more about this in Chapter Six. But first I have to write about my family left behind in Würzburg.

CHAPTER FIVE

THE FAMILY 1941-1943 – THE FAMILY'S DEPORTATION AND DEATH

Following my father's death, the family had to move to a very small flat, and then to the Jewish Old People's Home. This was where people were assembled for the deportation trains. Mother agreed to go with the Nazi drivers, or sometimes alone, into the villages of the region, to collect elderly Jews for deportation from Würzburg station. Here is a letter she wrote to Gustel Hess on one such journey:

Postmarked Bamberg, 8.6.42

Just now I passed through Schweinfurt and looked in your direction, now past Mainberg, do you remember the last time we went there for coffee? It was on 19 October 1940. In the train one is so wonderfully alone and inside the landscape. I have something to do in Hassfurt and am taking an afternoon to visit the grandparents, to see them once more [they were deported to Bamberg early in 1942]. Back tomorrow early on the 7 a.m. train. Tuesday probably very early to the Rhön, to fetch someone. Far to the north to Oberelsbach; once I went by car in the evening to Nordheim, your old district, that really is a mountain area. Once too in Hüttenheim, lastly to the Iffigheim mountain.

Just now Obertheres, where my great-grandfather lived – but this too an impressive scene, the whole range of the

Steigerwald in the noonday heat.

Now too the end has come for our use of the delightful Hess garden [belonging to a relative of Gustel], only this week is left. It's good that we still have the woods; it was wonderful yesterday afternoon with the children, singing rounds. Michael, however, did not come; he prefers to do jobs in the house, kitchen, cellar, in dirty blue overalls, happy being active and useful. We were at the place where the cowslips grow, now the blue columbine is glowing and a little deer was nibbling the tips of the larch trees. Almost every week, and each time different and wonderful. We really must make the most of it while we still have it, the time will soon come to an end.

How are you two? [Gustel and her mother].

Warmest greetings, R

Being herself obliged to take part in the deportation process, Mother was clearly aware that her family's turn would come. Note no names are given, to prevent identification.

My mother, brother and sister spent the last period of their lives at 6 Bibrastrasse, The Jewish Old People's Home, where the last remaining Jews of Würzburg were made to live under one roof. Before this the family had lived at 20 Dürerstrasse. Letters from my mother's friends after the war gave much information about this time and Frau Tony Schöffel, Gustel's cousin, also sent me letters after Gustel's death. For example, Anna Valeton wrote to Gustel on 11 December 1941, just after Father's death, saying that Mother was to be given a manager's position in the Home. She said Mother would be so very happy to see Gustel once more, for after her move that would be forbidden. Other documents show that the move did not take place immediately, but certainly before 8 June 1942, when the letter was written in the train.

Gustel's long letter of 1946 written to Uncle Leo says that she did manage to meet Mother in spite of the prohibition, in a little valley near Heidingsfeld, found by Cilly Bodky. Almost every week, early on Sunday, the friends would meet there and walk through the Guttenberg woods. There were severe penalties for Germans found associating with Jews, and, as Anna Valeton wrote to me (5 October 1946), the punishment would have been even worse for Mother. But her friends took risks gladly in their loyalty to her and the children, and all speak of her courage and serenity.

Within the Home, Mother was greatly helped by friendship with two Jewish families called Stahl and Schwab. She felt herself drawn to Henny Stahl as to a sister, and Herr Stahl said to Gustel, when she visited at night, that he was determined to look after Mother and the children as long as he could. The children were loved by everyone. Michael, aged ten in 1941, wanted to protect Mother after Father's death; at the same time he kept himself busy helping in the house. Lies, aged five, was showered with affection.

Writing about these terrible years for my family, I yet feel comforted to know they were surrounded by loving friends, and am deeply grateful to all who took the trouble, in spite of facing loss and danger themselves, to save letters, photos and some family mementoes for me.

* * *

The Nazi policy of eliminating the Jews had continued to grow steadily ever since *Kristallnacht* and the outbreak of war in 1939. On 20 January 1942, the Nazi leaders held a conference at Wannsee near Berlin, where Reinhard Heydrich, the leader responsible for Jewish policy, proposed the 'Final Solution' to the Jewish problem. This was to establish concentration camps, to which Jews would be sent on the pretence that they would be made to work. Only the fittest would be allowed to work, the rest would be killed. The Nazi leaders agreed to this plan, and proceeded to put it into effect. There had already been camps at

Dachau and Buchenwald, both in Germany. But the German army's conquests in eastern Europe meant that more camps could be established there. The name Auschwitz (Polish: Oswiecim) in Poland has come to stand for the full horror of the Nazi extermination policy.

The book *A History of The Holocaust*, by David Cesarani, published by The Holocaust Educational Trust (1995), gives maps and details of the murders carried out in these camps. On page 15 it states that: "hundreds of thousands of *non*-Jews were sent by the Nazis to concentration camps: anti-Nazis, Jehovah's Witnesses, homosexuals, the mentally ill and the chronically sick. In addition, more than 250,000 Gypsies were murdered, in a Nazi attempt to eliminate Gypsies as well as Jews from the map of Europe."

My grandparents were deported in September 1942 from Bamberg to the concentration camp at Theresienstadt (Czech: Terezín), in what was then Czechoslovakia. Josef was eighty-one, Rosette seventy-seven years old. The cruelty of uprooting two peaceful old people after a lifetime of work and bringing up a family is beyond words. Josef died there on 24 September 1942, and Rosette on 27 January 1943. I do not know if they were actually murdered, but deportation to such a place at their age was bound to lead to an early death.

Great-Aunt Helene was not mentioned by Uncle Leo after the war in his account of the grandparents' deaths, so I do not know what happened to her.

In 1943, after hearing nothing directly from my mother for years, I received three Red Cross letters from her. These were small printed forms conveyed between countries at war by the International Red Cross Organization. They contained basic details like the date, the sender, the addressee, and space for a short message. Mother's third letter, sent in June 1943, said "Tomorrow we are travelling to the East." It was the last letter I received. At the time I probably did not realize the significance of her words. But the last train deporting Jews left Würzburg on

17 June 1943, and documents still kept in the city's state archives show that my mother, brother and sister were on board. Again, I have to thank Professor Vollrath for sending me copies.

The overall instructions for deportations from the Reich Security Head Office in Berlin are dated 20 February 1943, and headed: "Guidelines for practical measures for the evacuation of Jews *to the East* (concentration camp Auschwitz)". So the destination is clearly stated here, but the police carrying out this "evacuation" are told (p. 5) not to mention it, but to note in the police register that the persons concerned have left for an "unknown destination".

Another set of papers contains secret plans for the train of 17 June 1943, part of it going to the concentration camp for old people at Theresienstadt, the rest to Auschwitz, but this is called "to the East", as required by the instructions quoted above. All the inhabitants of the Home and any other remaining Jews are listed.

The people concerned were given detailed instructions about how to prepare themselves and their belongings for the journey. According to the pretence that they were being sent East to work, Mother was instructed to provide per person:

Food for 5 days	2 sets of sheets
2 woollen blankets	1 eating bowl
1 suitcase or rucksack	1 mug
1 pair heavy work boots	1 spoon
2 pairs socks	2 shirts
2 pants	1 pullover
1 work garment	

Mother's friend, Cilly Bodky, in a long letter after the war, described among much other information how she helped Mother to prepare for the deportation. Cilly herself was half-

Jewish, but was apparently free to move about during these years:

Würzburg 30.9.46

Dear Hannah,

At last a letter from you has arrived. [After the end of the war, the friends had lost my address during the bombing of Würzburg, and I did not have their addresses.]

I only wish I could tell you something positive about your dear family. I was together with them until the last moment, that is, in 6 Bibrastrasse [the Home], and when the train left on 17.6.43 at 2.30 p.m. in the direction of Nuremberg, I waved to them from the Jewish cemetery.

[Cilly and other friends suspected that the worst had happened to those sent away, but were not able to find any definite information.] I can assure you of one thing, that they led a comparatively good life in Würzburg until the last day... Lies was too young to understand the position… and was excited about the long journey. Michael, so like his father… never said a word about the situation, a sure sign that he understood it. Your dear mother always accepted everything with such a calm spirit, in a way that is found only rarely in truly great people... So the last week before they left we were together every night sewing, trying on, packing and re-packing. At this time we had to be very careful [not to be found together].

I wish you from my heart all that is good and hope you will write soon.

Loving greetings from your Cilly.

The book about the Jews of Würzburg by Roland Flade describes the departure of the train on 17 June 1943. As a result of his research he points out (pp. 358–9) that detailed records of all those arriving at Auschwitz were normally kept at the office of the entry camp, where people were housed at first. Since none of the passengers on this train were named as having arrived, whereas they were fully listed at the Würzburg end, he concludes they must all have been sent straight to the gas chambers.

I have never been able to find any other definite information concerning the fate of my mother, brother and sister. After the war I sent a search questionnaire to the Red Cross, who could not tell me anything. Cilly Bodky once met a man who had survived Auschwitz and thought my family had died there, but without evidence. At the Polish State Memorial Museum, established at Auschwitz in 1947, the archivist Danuta Czech was given the task of compiling a *Calendar of Events in the Concentration Camp Auschwitz-Birkenau from 1939-1945*. A German translation of her monumental and harrowing work was kindly sent to me in 1989 by Frau Ingeborg Rose of Hamburg. The book lists all victims, but my family's names are not included. Danuta Czech mentions in her Introduction that some prisoners were sent to the gas chambers without being registered.

So I have to accept this conclusion. The horror of their deaths can only be imagined by those of us who survived. The utter madness of the Nazi extermination policies was not fully realized in Western countries until after Germany's defeat and the end of World War II in Europe on 8 May 1945. People who survived the camps have written about their experiences, and many historians have studied the Holocaust. Here I am writing what I have learnt about members of my immediate family. My oldest aunt, Martha, had fled with her husband and grown-up daughters to Holland. He died a normal death there, but she and her daughters Lisi and Lotte were sent to Auschwitz. Ruth Levinger, the daughter of my second aunt, Lieschen, had to go into a mental institution during the Nazi period. She did not survive, and the family believes that she was the victim of the policy that not only targeted the Jews, but singled out people with a mental handicap.

The question of whether the German people knew about the death camps has been discussed again and again. As we saw earlier, the regime established an all-encompassing hold on the population almost from the start. Yet some brave individuals did act publicly to declare their resistance to Hitler. This will be described in the next chapter. The courage and self-sacrifice of such people show that decency and humanity did survive in Germany in a very few instances. My parents' friends risked their own safety by helping the family, or simply by meeting them after it had been strictly forbidden. Yet unutterable crimes *were* committed. We can never again allow any ideology to murder people on account of their race or their political beliefs, or to do away with them because they do not fit a predetermined stereotype. Racism must be outlawed throughout the world.

Chapter Six

My Later School Years – The Last Period of the War

During the remaining years of the war I knew little of the fate of my family. Isolated cards or letters from Holland, the USA and Switzerland, especially in earlier years, had given some news and there was even post forwarded from Würzburg, but later there seemed to be no means of communicating with Germany, apart from Red Cross letters. Here is a letter from Aunt Lisel, wife of my uncle Leo, who had emigrated with him and Uncle Max to California, USA. She wrote to me regularly, and although they were always short of money, they generously sent me parcels or money for clothes:

Los Angeles, 10 July 1943

My dear good Hannah,

Warmest thanks for your kind, detailed letter of 22 May. This has more than made up for the long wait. And just think, it only took ten days!

I wanted to write to you much sooner, but had a lot to do...

We were so pleased that you heard from Mutti direct [via the Red Cross]. And how happy she will be when she hears from you...

We must all be comforted to know that dear Grandfather has finally been released from his great suffering... In earlier times we would have been sad about it, but today we can only thank God for taking him into His keeping. We only have to be sad about the tragedy he had to endure at his age, with dear Grandmother. We wonder how she is? We can only pray and hope that peace will come soon, to free them all and reunite us again.

Dear little Hannah, I know we don't need to worry about you. You are with good and kind people, and near to your mother and the little ones. And when the terrible war is over, you can be the first to see them again. That helps to make it easier for you...

I was so pleased that Anne [Hilb] heard from her mother. I think of her so often.

It is kind of you to ask about my own family [a Gentile family in Germany]. My dear mother unfortunately died two years ago, much too young. I did not want to tell you at the time. Yet I am thankful that she did not have to experience all the horrors the war has brought. For more than two years now I have heard nothing from my sister and my father...

The Red Cross letters to you only take three months [from Germany], so please let us know as soon as you hear from Mutti again...

Now you will be in the middle of exams, little Hannah, and I'll cross my fingers for you until 22 July. But I know you will do well. So, good luck, my dear!

We shall send some money to you this week, and hope you can buy something useful with it.

Many greetings from us to Nell, and to you warmest greetings and kisses from us all.

Your Auntie Lisel

These loving letters meant a great deal to me. There were also letters from Cousin Hanna, now in the USA with her husband and baby, and Cousin Lore in Switzerland. As Lisel's letter makes clear, we were all looking out for news, and did our best to keep in touch. But sadly, information available later shows that my mother probably, and my grandmother certainly, had died by the time this letter was written.

It was not until the end of the war that the horror of the concentration camps became generally known and I received the letters from my parents' friends in Germany, quoted in previous chapters. The fact that I was now a stateless person, and probably an orphan, did not really strike me until after I left school and went away to university. The kind and all-embracing guardianship of Nell Gill, together with the school staff and many others, took it for granted that I should be educated and encouraged to find a new identity. I was very much aware of their trust in me, and saw it as my duty to work hard and gain qualifications. It is only in recent years, meeting other lone refugee 'children' who had entered Britain via the *Kindertransports*, and hearing about their lives, that I have fully realized how very fortunate I was.

For the School Certificate examination (now GCSE) in 1943, I took English Language, English Literature, Mathematics, General Science, French, Latin, German, Music and Geography. The science was divided into three parts, Physics, Chemistry and Biology, none of which could be studied in any depth in the time available, but provided a helpful introduction. We also took lessons in History, Art, Religious Education, Gymnastics and Games. I was never much good at hockey or tennis, being rather a big girl and slow to move, but netball was a little better. The schoolwork came first, and I achieved a good examination result.

For Higher School Certificate (now Advanced Level), choices had to be made about a possible career. I was much involved in music and would have loved to take this up professionally, but had to admit that my standard of playing was not really high enough. Languages seemed the best bet. Earlier in the war, the school had appointed a German teacher to start up this subject. It now occurs to me that in the middle of the war against Germany, Italy and Japan, where Germany was seen as the chief enemy, the school acted courageously in this appointment, realizing that in the future it would be more than ever necessary to train people to become fluent in the German language and have some understanding of that country.

Since coming to England in 1939, I had had very little opportunity to speak German. Nell did know some German, but daily life during the war left no time to use it for conversation; in fact it was thought that in my own interests I should concentrate on English. Letters, and visits to the Valentin cousins in Croydon, helped me to keep some German going, but it was rather basic. This neglect of my native language was another aspect of my loss of identity, which was a real, though unacknowledged, part of my situation, in spite of all the kindness shown to me. So when German lessons were started at school, I experienced a great surge of recognition. It was like drawing words and sentences up from a deep well where they had lain dormant until needed. I was happy to find I could speak and write German fluently again, though my vocabulary, having remained at the level of a child of eleven, required a good deal of enlargement. I was thrilled to study some works of German literature, and saw them in part as a link with my parents, who would have known them too.

* * *

At various times during the war I was able to see a few relatives and friends from Germany. The Valentin family had emigrated to England before war began. Fritz Valentin was a second cousin of my mother. He and his wife Cili had three daughters, Ursula, Renate and Eva, and they lived in a flat in south London made available by the Society of Friends (Quakers). Fritz, though qualified as a lawyer in Germany, was unable to work professionally in England. So they had little money, but were always most generous to me, inviting me twice to visit them for Christmas. This was usually the time when I missed my own family most, and it meant a lot to spend

Christmas with them, in the way we had done at home.

My cousin Adolf was serving with the British Armed Forces, so I only saw him once during the war, when Nell invited him to Bristol for a weekend. Anne Hilb (who later sent me the moving letters from her mother, see pp. 71-73), was working in a hospital in Oxford, training to be a dietician. She had to attend evening classes as well, in order to pass the English school-leaving examinations, since the German ones were not recognized in this country. Nell invited her at least once; also she gave us a delicious evening meal, when we cycled from Bristol via Oxford to visit Nell's parents in Buckinghamshire.

Once Nell's parents had moved out of London to escape the wartime bombing, they lived in a centuries-old thatched cottage in a village called Aspley Guise (now part of the city of Milton Keynes). At Christmas and in the school holidays, I was always made welcome, together with Nell's sisters Mary, Connie, the twins Edie and Addie, and their young brother Bill, when he was on leave from the army. When Bill married Peggy in 1941, I was invited to be one of the bridesmaids. Nell's parents, Alice and Horace ('Auntie' and 'Uncle' to me), and the whole family were as generous as Nell herself in receiving me into their family circle.

In the summer holidays the school organized Harvest Camps in the Cotswold area, at various farms near the town of Cirencester. Many farm workers had been called up to join the forces, so schools were encouraged to help, especially with the potato harvest. We slept in large army tents and the teachers cooked on large outdoor stoves. It must have been a great deal of work for them, but apart from gathering in the potatoes, we had a lot of fun, singing folk songs and rounds, and cycling on Sundays round the lovely countryside. On one such occasion, my friend Olwen and I saw a strange apparition moving towards us: two ghostly figures with white helmets and enormous hands, and seemingly nothing else. Coming closer, they revealed themselves as two military policemen with white gauntlets on black motorcycles, preceding a large old-fashioned Rolls Royce in which an old lady sat, bolt upright, wearing a small, round flowery hat. It was Queen Mary, mother of the King, George VI; she was known to be spending the war years in Gloucestershire.

The harvest camps gave us the chance to spend weeks in the peaceful countryside, away from the danger of bombing. Fresh air, outdoor work, and clear starry skies at night were all part of this time. Friendships formed at school could be strengthened, and some, with Olwen Phillips, Monica Williams and Gwyneth Hughes, have lasted throughout my life.

* * *

Music formed a large part of my school life. As soon as I was competent enough on the cello, I joined the school orchestra, a very modest group numbering about four violins, one viola, one cello, piano and wooden recorders. However, there were two youth orchestras in Bristol which I joined as well, giving the opportunity of playing in a much larger ensemble. When I had been playing cello for about a year, one of these orchestras gave a concert in the spacious Colston Hall in central Bristol. In the next day's evening paper there was a report of this event, complete with a photograph of myself with long black plaits, holding cello and bow, and the caption: "She plays the low notes." Not world fame exactly, but encouraging.

In my senior years I was a member of the school choir, and occasionally sang Elizabethan madrigals with a few of the teachers. This glorious music of the sixteenth century was a pleasure to sing, so varied and subtle, joyful and melancholy by turns. I had responsibilities too. Apart from the classes for schoolwork, we were divided vertically for non-academic purposes into 'Houses', which competed against one another in sport, drama and music. So in my last year it fell to me to prepare and rehearse the short competition recital. This involved quite a lot of work, for we were limited to the few players fit to appear in a small chamber music ensemble in public. I chose the pieces and then had to arrange and sometimes transpose the music to suit the available instruments, a rewarding task when the result made something like a pleasing sound.

In the early war years the symphony orchestra of the BBC moved to Bristol to escape the air raids in London. They gave regular concerts and it was by attending these that I came to know the great works of the classical music repertoire. What a joy it was, then, to be selected to attend one of the first national orchestral courses for school pupils. This took place at Sherborne, Dorset in 1944 and again in 1945, and Mary Gill, a keen amateur player herself, helped to pay the fees. The excitement of playing in a full-size orchestra is something I shall never forget. Beethoven's Piano Concerto no. 3, marches by Elgar, dances by Delius were on the menu, not counting Schubert's Trout Quintet in the afternoons, and the chance to make new friends. We were immersed in the music, totally absorbed in getting it right, in answering the other instruments when our turn came, drawn into a greater whole. It is a unique experience.

* * *

Thanks to much hard work by the teachers and myself, I was able to take the Higher School Certificate (now called Advanced Level) in 1944, only one year after School Certificate, in German, French and Latin. During the following year I applied for a place at university, while continuing to study, and also working as Deputy Head Girl of the school. I was awarded a residential place at Westfield College, University of London, together with a small scholarship, to start in October 1945. That I was enabled to accept this place was due to grants, co-ordinated by Nell, from the City of Bristol, The Bristol Council for Refugees, a small grant from Redland High School, and help from the Refugee

Fund of Westfield College. In the circumstances I could not have expected to go to university at all: I shall never cease to be grateful to those who made it possible.

In summer 1944 the Allied Forces were preparing for a major attack from Britain on German-occupied France. For weeks beforehand, American troops were stationed in Bristol. Some were waiting for transport outside our school, under the lime trees forming an avenue up to the ornamental iron gates. When I walked along the avenue carrying my cello, there were calls of "Give us a tune" which I soon learnt to answer. What struck me about these soldiers was that they were not handsome film stars, such as we had seen in the cinema, but quite ordinary-looking men, some middle-aged, who had travelled across the dangerous Atlantic, infested with German U-boats, to help the Allied cause.

Was there no resistance to Hitler *within* Germany? Sophie and Hans Scholl, a brother and sister who were students at the University of Munich, decided that they had to stand up to the Nazis, regardless of the danger to themselves. They mounted a protest campaign by means of secretly printed leaflets, which they circulated and dropped on several occasions into the central hall of the university from the top of the staircase. A number of brave people joined their protest, but they were betrayed by the hall porter, tried, and executed on 22 February 1943 together with Christoph Probst. Fellow protesters were executed later that year.

By 1944, a larger plot against Hitler was taking shape, organized by disillusioned army officers and convinced Christians. The conspirators had laid plans to conceal a bomb in a briefcase, to be placed against the leg of a table at a meeting on 20 July 1944 where Hitler would be present. The bomb did go off, but on the far side of the table from Hitler, who was not hurt. Immediate arrests were made, followed by executions soon afterwards. One of the foremost Resistance figures was the Christian minister Dietrich Bonhoeffer, a leading spokesman for German Protestant opposition to the Nazi regime. He was active in ecumenical affairs and knew Bishop George Bell of Chichester. In 1942 he flew to Sweden to convey to the British government, through Bishop Bell, the proposals of the Resistance for a negotiated peace with the Western Allies. They, however, insisted on demanding the unconditional surrender of Germany. Bonhoeffer was arrested and imprisoned by the Nazis in 1943, and hanged in 1945.

The Allied invasion of France, starting with landings on the Normandy beaches on 6 June 1944, began a long campaign to drive the German army out of occupied Europe. In another part of the campaign, Allied forces were fighting their way north from the southern tip of Italy. Finally, the Russian army was advancing steadily from the east towards Berlin. By spring 1945 it was clear that Germany had lost the war. On 30 April 1945, Hitler committed suicide in Berlin. On 8 May, his successor, Admiral Dönitz, signed the armistice, conceding Germany's total surrender. Germany was in ruins, its cities bombed into rubble; the government had collapsed, the people had little food and often no fuel. As information about the Holocaust began to emerge, the sense of guilt, especially among the younger generation, added to the general feeling of desolation.

In Britain, the end of the war in Europe was greeted with huge relief. Families could look forward to their fighting men and women coming home; for Nell this meant her brother Bill, who had been fighting with the British army in Germany. On the day peace returned, there were flags waving, church bells ringing, and I saw people dancing in the streets. Those who had given their lives to defeat Nazism were not forgotten, but overall there was a sense that people could now get on with their ordinary lives, their hopes and plans again.

The war in the Far East, however, continued until after the dropping of the atomic bombs on Hiroshima and Nagasaki. Japan surrendered on 15 August 1945.

Chapter Seven

A Student in London – Paris and Bristol – Aubrey Hickman

In early October 1945, I arrived at Westfield College in London. The University of London is made up of separate colleges: at that time, Westfield was a small women's college situated in Hampstead; much later it amalgamated with Queen Mary College in East London. Westfield, like Redland High School in Bristol, had been founded in 1882 as part of the movement to provide higher education for women.

The subjects for my degree course were German with subsidiary French. Some people have been surprised that I should have chosen to study German, after the horrific things that had been done to my family. But in 1944, when this decision had to be made, I did not know of their fate. The teachers at school and I agreed that I would do best to study languages, and in that case it made sense to choose German, my native language. Over three years, the continual study of the German language and the best of German literature, much of which my parents had known, strengthened my sense of identity and continuity. I began to realize that after the terrible years of the war which had just ended, one of the most important tasks ahead was to work for international understanding.

Since the London regulations required four subjects at Higher School Certificate and I had only done three, I added English Literature for the first year. This meant a more intensive study of selected works than at school, which was very satisfying; two I remember were *Othello* by Shakespeare and *The Duchess of Malfi* by Webster. In German, a widespread knowledge of classical literature was required, Goethe and Schiller, the Austrian dramatist Grillparzer, and many others including one or two medieval texts. In French, we read works by Corneille, Racine and Molière, as well as nineteenth-century poetry. I was only seventeen and a half at the beginning of my course. It would have been possible to stay on at school for another year, but I had made up my mind to start earning my own living as soon as possible, to relieve the burden on Nell. So I was quite a lot younger than some other first-year students, who had received extra tuition at school. My lack of training in extensive literature studies became clear in the first few months, but by the end of the first year I had caught up. By studying literature we also gained insights into the historical and cultural backgrounds of the writers concerned, and thus some understanding of the development of each country.

At least half the time was taken up with language work: regular weekly translations into German or French, plus translations from them into English. We also studied the historical development of the German language, though not linguistics in today's sense of the word. However, there was much less practice in using the spoken language than nowadays. The regular translations, based on a wide variety of texts, presented a real and stimulating challenge. This was one of the best ways to gain a deep and wide knowledge of the subtleties of vocabulary, to acquire a feeling for the idiomatic characteristics of each language. It was worthwhile struggling for hours, surrounded by dictionaries, with Macbeth's speech beginning "Is this a dagger which I see before me?" if by the end one could achieve something that might be spoken by a German actor on a stage.

Since numbers of students taking German in the whole university were rather low, some of the work was organized to be done collectively at central colleges. Thus on Tuesdays we heard lectures at Bedford College in Regent's Park, on Wednesdays at King's College in the Strand, and on Thursdays at University College in Gower Street; seminars and essay work followed later. In addition to students straight from school like myself, there were a number of ex-Service students who had returned from war service, resulting in a fruitful mix of personalities and age groups.

* * *

The Principal of the college at this time was Mrs Mary Stocks. Herself a graduate in Economic and Social History, she had lived for years in Manchester where her husband was Professor of Philosophy. Having great faith in education and reform, she was a part-time lecturer and did social work among the poor families of central Manchester, while bringing up her own family. Later she worked as a magistrate. After her husband's death she became Principal of Westfield. We could not have had a better woman to preside over our college, and she cared about every student. When, in my second year, I founded a small college orchestra and shyly invited her to the opening concert, she came, striding along in her tweed suit, blue stockings and flat sandals. Never mind her university and government committees, if her students were doing something she believed in, she supported them. She was also actively interested in the refugee situation, and there were a number of refugee scholars on the staff.

In addition to conducting the college orchestra, I belonged to the University's choral society. I also joined a large orchestra for amateurs and music students, conducted at the Royal Academy of Music by one of its senior staff, Ernest Read. He had been involved in running the summer music courses I had attended previously, and some of the people I had met then were also in the orchestra; two of these were Margaret Rawling and Janet Craxton, later a famous oboist. We played mainly classical works, but also some Benjamin Britten; the standard was high for amateurs and a constant challenge to me. The rehearsals were a highlight of each week.

At college I made several friends. The one with whom I had most in common was Ray (Renate) Friedenthal, also a refugee, who was studying German like myself. Her family and she had become Christians. At weekends she could go home, as the family lived near London, and so did some other students I knew. So weekends were sometimes lonely for me, though brightened by occasional invitations to visit the cousins in Croydon. Cousin Adolf and his wife Ruth, now living in London, also invited me from time to time for Sunday lunch, and I appreciated their kindness.

On days when I found myself alone, I was conscious all the more of missing my immediate family and kept wondering what had become of them. I was grateful to my parents' friends for their letters describing the family's life, but they had no information as to what had happened later. The Red Cross was unable to help. In the immediate post-war years, eastern Europe was full of displaced persons, often being moved from one camp to another, so it was difficult to trace anyone. The United Nations set up a relief organization, and in my final university year I applied for a post to work with them, hoping that this would also help me to find out about my family. But at the interview I was told kindly but firmly that anyone sent by them would have to be at least 25 (I was just 20), and with training as a teacher or a social worker. So I made other plans, always hoping that if my family had survived, they would contact me, since they knew where I was.

Here I would like to say a few words about my cousins, the Valentins, and what happened to them after the war. Fritz, although of Jewish background, had been baptized as a baby; his wife Cili was a Christian without any Jewish connections. Fritz explained much later that in spite of being persecuted by the Nazis and forced into exile, he had never denied his allegiance to the true German people, for whom he had fought and worked as a younger man. Once the war was over, he decided it was his duty to return to Hamburg, which had been heavily bombed, to help in the reconstruction of normal life after the Nazi nightmare. With great courage he returned early in 1946, when things were very bad in his home city and there was little food, to work as a lawyer and then a judge. His wife and younger daughters, Renate and Eva, followed in the summer of 1947. Their eldest daughter Ursula stayed in England with her English husband Arthur.

In 1947 I was able to become a naturalized British citizen. This involved taking an oath of allegiance to the King. I was very grateful for the privilege of citizenship and the chance to apply for a British passport. It meant that I was no longer a stateless person, but someone with the right to a home in the country that had saved my life. It implied too that one should try to be a good citizen, an obligation especially present in the minds of those who have not enjoyed the rights of citizenship from birth.

One of the college societies I joined was the Student Christian Movement. Even at school I had taken part in religious discussion groups, being increasingly aware of a vacuum in my personal religious life. The school and Westfield College were run on Christian lines, with morning prayers every day; Nell was a Christian believer, but she never tried to influence me. I came to believe that the Christian religion was a natural follow-up of the Jewish religion. After much thought, reading and discussion, I decided to be baptized and become a Christian.

All through the war I had corresponded regularly with my relatives in America, seeing such letters as real though indirect contact with my parents, brother and sister. Even when those who were in America lost contact with Germany, they were still part of my family. After the end of the war, when there was no news and we had to face the fact that the family in Germany might not have survived, the links with America became, if anything, more important. When I told Uncle Leo that I was thinking of becoming a Christian, he replied at once. In a long, serious letter he warned me to reconsider, not to make a hasty decision or cut myself off from the Jewish faith and community. But the fact was that as child in Germany I had not been brought up as a practising Jew. I felt and still do feel a Jewish person, but through the years in England I had become drawn into the Christian community and learned to accept the teachings of Jesus. Many years later, Nell told me that my mother had written to her expressing the hope that I would become a Christian, but Nell had not told me this at the time, allowing me to reach my own decision.

Once the decision was made, the question was: which denomination should I join? Every Sunday I attended a different service in London, trailing from the Catholics to the Baptists, the Quakers to the Anglicans. It was all very confusing. Finally, a young Canadian Presbyterian minister, who sometimes came to the Student Christian Movement meetings at College, suggested I could be baptized at his church, and if I chose to move on later, no hard feelings. So this is what happened. I was baptized in London, but two years later, while studying in Bristol, I joined the Church of England, largely because I felt more at home with its form of service, including so much beautiful music.

* * *

I obtained my degree in 1948. By this time I had become very interested in German studies, and would have liked to do research for a higher degree. But grants were few, and without a grant there was no question of continuing in this direction. So I decided to enrol for a concentrated teacher training year, financially supported by the government. My course, at the University of Bristol, was to begin in autumn 1949. Thus there was a year free to do other things. The main priority, as I saw it, was to spend time in France, to improve my command of the language and get to know the country and its people.

As a result of contacts made by friends, I was invited to work as an au pair girl at the home of Monsieur and Madame Doreau in Paris, from autumn 1948. They had eight children and lived in a large flat in the Rue de Grenelle, not far from the Eiffel Tower. The two eldest children were at boarding school. My time was largely spent with the boy of five, Gillou, and the girl aged three, Sylvie. I was expected to wash and dress them in the morning and get them ready for bed at night, escort the five-year-old to and from kindergarten, and help in other ways. Sometimes I took the baby and the little girl for walks in the park under the Eiffel Tower or along the banks of the Seine nearby.

Although I had studied French language and literature at school and university, it was quite another matter to understand small children or to communicate in shops, on buses and so on. Madame treated me with great kindness. The arrangement was that in return for my work, I received board and lodging. There was no actual pay, but I ate the same food as the family and together with them, which was not always the case for au pair girls. Every now and then Madame would give me a ticket for the theatre or opera. It was marvellous to see one of the great plays by Racine, which I had read at university, brought to life by the finest actors in France. On the other hand, there was a farce by Feydeau, first performed in 1907, which had the audience roaring with laughter. Bizet's opera *Carmen* also proved to be an unforgettable experience.

Two mornings a week I attended lectures at the University of the Sorbonne, founded in the thirteenth century. In the course of these visits I made friends with a French girl, and one bitterly cold Sunday in January we set off by train to visit the cathedral of Chartres, one of the finest Gothic churches in the world. The medieval stained-glass windows glow with intense colours, chiefly blues and reds. Each of the larger windows was the gift of one of the medieval guilds, who placed a 'signature' picture at the bottom. I bought a photo of one showing a waggoner with his horse and cart. An artist friend copied it on a larger scale, and it now hangs in my house. On other Sundays I was free to explore the buildings and museums of Paris. The whole period remains in my mind as one of steady work in a friendly family, while gaining knowledge of the riches of French culture. By the time I left, my spoken French had improved considerably.

In October 1949 I was back in Bristol to study for the Postgraduate Certificate in Education. I lived in Nell's flat again, but the government grant for teacher training enabled me to pay my way. The course was organized to have lectures and written work in the autumn term, supervised teaching practice in schools in the spring term, and more lectures and writing between Easter and the examination. The lectures ranged from the history of education to discussions about teaching methods, in my case for modern languages. One of the most interesting topics was child psychology, necessary for teachers and useful later, when I had children of my own. By the end of the course I was a qualified teacher.

* * *

In the summer of 1946, after my first year at university, Cousin Lore had invited me to visit her in Switzerland. Being a neutral country, Switzerland had attracted thousands of refugees from Germany and Austria during the Nazi period. Since I was still a stateless person in 1946, the Swiss authorities demanded that Lore should deposit a sizeable sum of money, partly to guarantee my return fare to England, before they would grant me an entry visa. Lore somehow managed to raise this amount, and then I was told to wait. I waited and waited. After six weeks, a letter arrived demanding that I too should pay a similar deposit. By this time I had had enough. It was out of the question for me to find a large sum of money at short notice in addition to the grants I was receiving for my education. I withdrew my visa application and told Lore I could not come.

What now? I knew that a music course was about to start, which I could pay for instead of the fare to Switzerland. One of the organizers told me there were still vacancies, so off I went. It was a singing course held near Newbury in Berkshire, with madrigals and choral works. It was here that I met Aubrey Hickman. He had been serving with the Royal Navy during the war, and had left in 1945 to continue his university course. Since we were both studying in London and members of the university choral society, we met about once a week in term-time. Although there were quite long periods when we could not meet, the friendship lasted, and we became engaged in 1948.

Aubrey Hickman was born in Chelmsford on 2 April 1922. His parents, John and Eleanor Hickman, were Londoners but had moved to Chelmsford during the First World War. John had volunteered for the army, but had been rejected on account of his deformed feet, the result of his impoverished childhood. At about this time he also suffered a serious attack of pneumonia. So they moved to Chelmsford, then a small town, where Eleanor's family lived, and where John worked as a foreman storekeeper at the ball-bearing factory of Hoffmann.

Eleanor did well enough at elementary school to win a scholarship to continue her education. However, her parents had 11 children, so she was expected to find work as soon as possible. For a time she was a maid in the home of an aristocratic family, at another stage she worked in a factory making sweets. John and Eleanor married in 1912 and had two older children when Aubrey was born, John (b. 1914) and Doris (b. 1916).

Eleanor knew all the music-hall songs of her youth and sang them round the house. All the family were musical, and the two boys belonged to the choir of St Peter's Church, whose organist, William Bush, was in charge of Dace's music shop in the town. Although Aubrey had several periods of ill health as a child, his musical ability was exceptional and he was a highly gifted violinist. Mr Bush provided encouragement, harmony and organ lessons, and paid for violin lessons at an increasingly high standard. When Aubrey won a scholarship to the local grammar school at the age of 11 (1933), he made new musical friends and played in an orchestra for the first time. Other subjects also required hard work, but with two hours of violin practice daily, plus choir duties, he had a very full timetable.

Some people expected Aubrey to aim for a career as a solo violinist, but he himself wanted to become a composer. So in 1940, having won a County Scholarship, he began studies for a humanities degree (Music, English and Latin), intending to specialize in music later. He was at University College, University of London, evacuated during the war to Southampton.

By 1942, when Britain had been at war for three years, he joined the Royal Naval Volunteer Reserve as a temporary Sub-Lieutenant. Aubrey had always taken an active interest in amateur radio, encouraged by his father, whom he remembered as a skilled, if unqualified, engineer. John Hickman could, for example, carry out detailed maintenance of his motorbike, and was enthusiastic about the new possibilities of 'wireless'. Marconi's Wireless Telegraph and Signal Company, the first wireless factory in the world, had been established in Chelmsford in 1898, and it was here that Eleanor's father worked. Aubrey's father constructed simple wireless receivers. Aubrey was a constant helper in his father's enterprises, and one of his earliest memories was of hearing voices from the transmitter at nearby Writtle through headphones attached to a crystal set.

When Aubrey applied to join the Royal Naval Reserve, his scientific knowledge led to a six-month training course to become a Naval Radar Officer. Radar, a method of locating objects by use of high-powered radio pulses, had been developed to detect the movement of enemy aircraft. Its use in ships was relatively new, and Aubrey joined only the second group of trainees for this work. He was stationed at Rosyth Naval Base in Scotland, and over the next three years was responsible for servicing and repairing the radar apparatus of destroyers operating in the

North Sea. The ships usually came into port, but sometimes he had to go out to sea in all kinds of weather. He told me that at least once he had had to step across from one destroyer to another, a hazardous undertaking even if the weather had been calm. He was commended by the Commander-in-Chief for "exceptional zeal and devotion to duty".

In October 1945 he resumed his studies at London University. Having completed his degree, he transferred in 1947 to the Royal Academy of Music in London for a Licentiate course in Composition and Viola. In 1949 he was awarded the premier prize for composition and a prize for string quartet playing, as well as graduating from his course.

We were married in 1950, and over the next six years had two sons and a daughter. After the sadness of losing my immediate family, after the dangers Aubrey had faced in the war, we were thankful for this new family and the hope it gave us for the future.

Epilogue

Our first home was in New Mills near Stockport, where Aubrey taught music at the grammar school, while continuing his own studies. I taught French and German at the grammar school for girls in Buxton, until our first child was born. In 1952 Aubrey was awarded an external music degree of the University of Durham. We then moved to Belfast, Northern Ireland, where he became a lecturer at a large teacher training college. Two more children were born here, so for some years I was fully occupied at home.

In 1959 Aubrey became a lecturer at the University of Manchester. He also embarked on research for a doctorate degree, concentrating on the psychology of music. This was a rapidly developing area of research in which he played a leading role in Britain and internationally. The results of many experimental studies influenced the training of music teachers and opened up new directions for music education in schools.

I went back to teaching at two grammar schools in Altrincham, teaching some French but mainly German. More and more I found myself needing to understand the causes of Hitler's rise to power, which had had such a tragic effect on my family. Nell Gill's generosity again played a part in my next move: the West German government had paid me some compensation for the education I had missed by having to flee in 1939. Of course I gave this money to Nell, who generously gave it back to me, suggesting I might use it to fund some research. So I studied for a doctorate involving the historical background to Hitler, as well as literature of the period. The focus of my research was the Austrian writer Robert Musil, a contemporary of Hitler and of my father. I studied his first novel, which describes the development of identity in an alien environment, and in which I found some parallels with my own growing up. Musil's work as a whole touches on many ideas which have had a lasting influence in the twentieth century.

After completing this degree, I lectured in German at the Universities of Manchester and Salford. The aim of my work was always to bear witness to the Holocaust, but also to improve international relations by communicating the good aspects of German culture. I was constantly aware of the need for reconciliation with those Germans who did not support the Nazis, or who were born during or after the war. We visited Germany several times to see relatives returned from exile and to thank German friends who had stood by my parents during the dangerous years. My children played with German children, helping to contribute, if only in a small way, towards laying the foundations for international understanding. In 1996 I was invited as a former Jewish citizen of Würzburg to visit as a guest of the city; during this stay I was shown much kindness. I talked with senior pupils in two grammar schools, and their questions showed that they needed to come to terms with national crimes for which they were not responsible. They appreciated my open attitude and emphasis on working for the future together.

Nell Gill lived until 1999. Her life was full and productive in many fields, and she extended her love and caring to our whole family. I remember with deepest gratitude that she saved me from the Nazis and brought me up as her own daughter; without her, I would not have survived.

My husband died in 1986. I am thankful for the years we had together, and for our children, now with families of their own. The fate of my parents, brother and sister is always in my thoughts. I hope they would have been glad to see new life arise after tragedy.

Acknowledgements

This book could not have been written without help from many people. I wish to thank the numerous friends and relatives who encouraged me to undertake this work, sometimes painful, but always necessary.

Many letters have contributed to the book. Letters were sent to me by my parents and other relatives in my first three months in England. Once the war had begun, the normal postal service from Germany was cut off. My cousin Lore Jacobsohn in Switzerland, which was neutral, my uncles Max and Leo Weinberger and Leo's wife Lisel in the USA, and later my cousin Hanna Naumann in the USA, sent me news of my family. Once America entered the war against Germany (December 1941), this became even more difficult. The Red Cross organized the sending of short messages, only twenty-five words on a printed form; my mother sent me three of these during the last months of her life.

After the war I received letters about my family from my parents' friends: Frau Anna Valeton and her husband Professor Josué Valeton; Fräulein Cilly Bodky (and photos); the sisters Fräulein Paula and Fräulein Martha Heine; the Bauer family, in whose house we had lived; the Pfeiffer family; Fräulein Gustel Hess, and others. Miss Anne Hilb and Mrs Leonore Veltfort née Valeton each sent me letters written by their mothers during the war. My cousins Lore and Hanna gave me information about the family, including our grandfather's *Memoir of My Life*, photos, and facts about our maternal ancestors researched by Herr Manfred Göske of Lüneburg. Frau Toni Schöffel sent letters and photos collected during the war by Gustel Hess. Frau Christa Stellman sent photos. Frau Heidi Gromes-Hechtel sent documents left by Frau Emmy Weinberger, widow of my uncle Max.

My cousin Ursula Windsor sent the text of a speech given by her father, Fritz Valentin. My cousin Ruth Verroen sent photos and letters, also a book about our family which was received after my book was completed.

The Mayor of Würzburg generously invited me for a visit in 1996 as guest of the city, during which I met the following people who were very helpful: Professor Hans-Joachim Vollrath, who gave me a book on Jewish religion and obtained many documents on my behalf; Dr Alexander von Papp, who gave me a book on the Jews of Würzburg on behalf of the city; Dr Hans-Peter Baum of the Jewish Documentation Centre in Würzburg, who sent much important information and Herr Paul Lesch of the Jewish Memorial Centre, Gaukönigshofen, who gave me information and a book.

Frau Ingeborg Rose of Hamburg gave me a detailed and harrowing book about the concentration camp at Auschwitz. Mr Trevor Mason of British Aerospace, Bristol, sent information on a tragic air raid in 1940. Professor Marie-Louise Roth sent me her book about her experiences during the war in a forced labour camp. Professor Franz Richter sent me the novel based on his war experiences in the German army. Professor Peter Skrine drew my attention to *A Bristolian and the Third Reich* by Margaret Goodbody, and Mrs Marjorie Cox to *Refugee Scholars*, edited by R. M. Cooper. Several friends and relatives gave me memoirs or novels of experiences during the Holocaust, including a book about resistance within Germany sent by my cousin Fritz Levinger and his wife Betty. I should like to express my warmest thanks to all of these.

I am most grateful for generous advice given by Professor Edward Timms of the Centre for German-Jewish Studies at the University of Sussex; by Ms Paula Kitching of the Holocaust Educational Trust; and by Dr Christina Ujma of the University of Loughborough. Dr Stephen Parker of the University of Manchester invited me to read from my book in the Department of German and the following discussion was most illuminating. Conversations with the Reverend Michael Robinson of St Peter's Church, Hale, furthered my understanding of the role of Dietrich Bonhoeffer during the war and were helpful in other ways. Mr Nick Turnbull made constructive comments on the text. Mrs Caroline Holmes helped me to find a way forward after serious illness.

My adoptive mother, the late Miss Nell Gill, always believed that my story should be told. My children and their families have constantly supported me in this work, and from the start my daughter Ruth offered constructive criticism and editorial advice. My friend Barbara Pearson generously took over the typing at a difficult time and helped me with moral support throughout; without her the book would not have been completed. To all these people I wish to express my deepest gratitude. Finally, may I express my deep appreciation to Dr. Stephen Smith and his staff at Beth Shalom Holocaust Centre, and Quill Press, for publishing the book. I am most grateful for their care, collaboration and devotion to the highest standards, which have been vital to producing such an excellent result.

Text acknowledgements: I should like to thank the following for permission to include quotations from restricted or published works: the *Staatsarchiv*, Würzburg, for permission to print two pages from my Gestapo file no. 16848 (Weinberger, Hanna); The Holocaust Educational Trust, London, for *A History of the Holocaust* by David Cesarani, edited by Jonathan Freedland and Jon Mendelson (1995).

Select Bibliography

a) Works in English

Cesarani, David, ed by Jonathan Freedland and Jon Mendelson, *A History of the Holocaust* (London, 1995).

Clare, George, *Last Waltz in Vienna: The Destruction of a Family 1842–1942* (London, 1981).

Cooper, R. M. (ed), *Refugee Scholars: Conversations with Tess Simpson* (Leeds, 1992).

Craig, Gordon A., *Germany 1866–1945* (Oxford, 1978).

Goodbody, Margaret, *A Bristolian and the Third Reich: Memoirs 1933–1948* (Bristol, 1991).

Kindertransport, Reunion of, *Sixtieth Anniversary of the Kindertransport 1939–1999* (London, 1999).

Kohn, Hans, *The Mind of Germany: The Education of a Nation* (London, 1961).

Leverton, Bertha and Shmuel Lowensohn (eds), *I Came Alone: The Stories of the Kindertransports* (Lewes, 1990).

Morgan, Roger (ed), *Germany 1870–1970: A Hundred Years of Turmoil* (London, 1970).

Musil, Robert, *Diaries 1899–1941*, ed. Mark Minsky, tr. Philip Payne (New York, 1998).

Passant, E. J., with W. O. Henderson, C. J. Child and D. C. Watt, *A Short History of Germany 1815–1945* (Cambridge, 1969).

Parkes, James, *A History of the Jewish People*, 2nd edn, (Harmondsworth, 1964).

Prater, Donald A., *European of Yesterday: A Biography of Stefan Zweig* (Oxford, 1972).

Richards, Denis, *Modern Europe 1789–1945*, 5th edn, (London, 1967).

Uris, Leon, *Exodus: A Novel of Israel* (London, 1959).

Zweig, Stefan, *The World of Yesterday, An Autobiography* [tr not given] (London, Toronto, Melbourne and Sydney, 1944).

Articles

Craig, Gordon A., "Becoming Hitler", Review Article on: *Hitler's Thirty Days to Power* by Henry Ashby Turner, Jr. (London, 1996); *Nazi Germany and the Jews: Volume One: The Years of Persecution, 1933–1939* by Saul Friedländer (London, 1997); *Confronting the Nazi Past: New Debates on Modern German History*, Michael Burleigh (ed), (New York, 1996), *New York Review of Books*, 29.5.1997, 7–11.

Craig, Gordon A., "Working Toward The Führer", Review Article on: *Germans into Nazis* by Peter Fritzsche (Cambridge MA USA, 1998); *Hitler, 1889–1936: Hubris* by Ian Kershaw, (London, 1998); *Hitler's Vienna: A Dictator's Apprenticeship* by Brigitte Hamann, tr. Thomas Thornton (Oxford, 1999); *Where Ghosts Walked: Munich's Road to the Third Reich* by David Clay Large (London, 1997), *New York Review of Books*, 18.3.1999, 32–35.

Gross, John, "A Nice Pleasant Youth", Review Article on: *Explaining Hitler: The Search for the Origins of His Evil* by Ron Rosenbaum (New York, 1998), *New York Review of Books*, 17.12.1998, 12–17.

b) Works in German

Chagall, Bella, *Brennende Lichter*, tr. from Yiddish by Lia Bernstein and Theodora von der Mühll (Reinbek bei Hamburg, 1966).

Conze, Werner und Volker Hentschel (eds) *Ploetz: Deutsche Geschichte. Epochen und Daten*, 4th edn (Darmstadt, 1988).

Czech, Danuta, *Kalendarium der Ereignisse im Konzentrationslager Auschwitz-Birkenau 1939–1945*, tr. from Polish by Jochen August, Nina Kozlowski, Silke Lent and Jan Parcer (Reinbek bei Hamburg, 1989).

Fischer, Brigitte B., *Sie schrieben mir oder was aus meinem Poesiealbum wurde* (München, 1981).

Flade, Roland, *Die Würzburger Juden, Ihre Geschichte vom Mittelalter bis zur Gegenwart.* Mit einem Beitrag von Ursula Gehring-Münzel (Würzburg, 1987).

Frank, Anne, *Das Tagebuch der Anne Frank 12. Juni 1942–1. August 1944*, tr. from Dutch by Anneliese Schütz (Frankfurt am Main und Hamburg, 1955).

Göpfert, Rebecca, *Der jüdische Kindertransport von Deutschland nach England 1938/39. Geschichte und Erinnerung* (Frankfurt am Main, 1999).

Huppert, Hilde, *Hand in Hand mit Tommy. Ein autobiographischer Bericht 1939–1945* (St. Ingbert, 1988).

Jäckel, Eberhard, *Hitlers Herrschaft*, 3rd edn (Darmstadt, 1991).

Musil, Robert, *Tagebücher*, hrsg. von Adolf Frisé (Reinbek bei Hamburg, 1976, 1983).

Richter, Franz, *Spaltklang: Roman vom Erbteil Europa* (St. Pölten-Wien, 1987).

Scholl, Inge, *Die weisse Rose* (Frankfurt am Main, 1953).

Sholom Alejchem, *Tevje, der Milchmann,* tr. from Yiddish by Alexander Eliasberg (Wiesbaden, 1960).

Staden, Wendelgard von, *Nacht über dem Tal. Eine Jugend in Deutschland* (Düsseldorf. Köln, 1979).

Valentin, Fritz, "Bewahrung der Heimat im Schicksal der Emigranten", speech on 9.November 1965 (anniversary of *Kristallnacht*), in: *Zeitschrift für Kirche und Judentum*, 1/68, Feb, 5ff.

Walter, Wolfgang, *Meinen Bund habe ich mit dir geschlossen. Jüdische Religion in Fest, Gebet und Brauch* (Leipzig, 1988)

Zuckmayer, Carl, *Als wär's ein Stück von mir. Horen der Freundschaft* (New York, 1966).

Zuckmayer, Carl, *Aufruf zum Leben. Porträts und Zeugnisse aus bewegten Zeiten* (Frankfurt am Main, 1976).

Zweig, Stefan, *Die Welt von Gestern. Erinnerungen eines Europäers* (Stockholm 1944).

Documents

Staatsarchiv Würzburg, Gestapostelle 16848,

WEINBERGER Hanna Gertrud Sara. Documents from this file were copied by special permission and kindly sent to me by Professor Hans-Joachim Vollrath, University of Würzburg.

In addition, Prof. Vollrath sent me copies of a number of Gestapo or similar documents not specific to one person. These include:

(a) directions from the Central State Security Office in Berlin concerning deportation of Jews to Auschwitz (20.2.1943);

(b) details concerning the final deportation train from Würzburg (17.6.1943), instructions for preparations by deportees and a list of passengers including my family;

(c) accounts for the money paid in by the Jews travelling on this and previous deportation trains and other relevant lists (papers dated 25.6.1943–8.8.1944).

c) Work in French

Roth-Zimmerman, Marie-Louise, *Je me souviens de Schelklingen: Une jeune Alsacienne dans un camp de rééducation nazi* (Strasbourg, 1999).